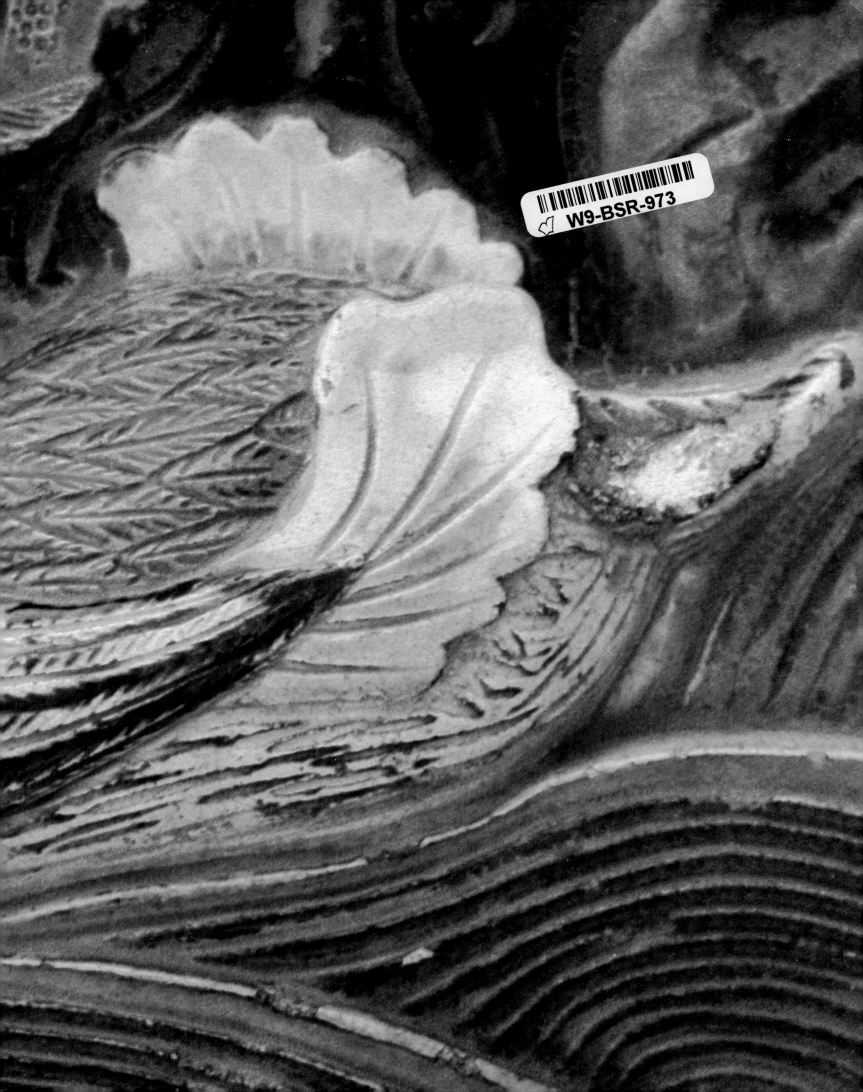

PEKING

By David Bonavia
and the Editors of Time-Life Books

Photographs by
Peter John Griffiths

THE GREAT CITIES · TIME-LIFE BOOKS · AMSTERDAM

The Author: David Bonavia was born in Aberdeen, Scotland, in 1940. After graduation from Cambridge University, where he took First Class Honours in Modern Languages and in Chinese, he worked as a journalist in Africa and Asia. He became Moscow correspondent for *The Times* of London in 1969, but was expelled from the U.S.S.R. in 1972 for his reporting on Soviet dissidents. His study of the Soviet protest movement, *Fat Sasha and the Urban Guerrilla*, was published soon afterwards. From 1972 to 1976 he was correspondent for *The Times* in Peking.

The Photographer: Peter John Griffiths was born in London in 1947 and studied Modern Chinese at Leeds University. He worked as a correspondent in Peking for two-and-a-half years and has photographed throughout South-east Asia and India.

EDITOR: George Constable
Assistant Editor: Kit van Tulleken
Design Consultant: Louis Klein
Chief Designer: Graham Davis
Director of Photography: Pamela Marke

Editorial Staff for Peking:
Deputy Editors: John Cottrell, Christopher Farman
Designer: Eric Molden
Picture Editor: Gunn Brinson
Staff Writers: Tony Allan, Mike Brown
Text Researcher: Jackie Matthews
Design Assistants: Steve Duwensee, Martin Gregory, Fiona Preston

Editorial Production for the Series:
Art Department: Julia West
Editorial Department: Ellen Brush, Ajaib Singh Gill
Picture Department: Thelma Gilbert, Brigitte Guimpier

The captions and text of the picture essays were written by the staff of TIME-LIFE Books.

Published by TIME-LIFE International (Nederland) B.V. Ottho Heldringstraat 5, Amsterdam 1018.

Cover: Golden-yellow palace and temple roofs in the heart of Peking blaze against a summer sky. During the city's imperial past, tiles of this colour appeared only on buildings into which the emperor might set foot.

First end paper: Fired in delicate shades of green and ivory, a ceramic mandarin duck—a species traditionally symbolic of marital fidelity—floats upon the stylized waves of a tiled screen in the imperial gardens of Peking's Forbidden City. Screens were placed in front of entranceways to keep out malevolent spirits, which supposedly could move only in straight lines.

Last end paper: Ranks of neatly aligned and nearly identical bicycles—Peking's prime mode of transport—fill a city-centre parking lot. There are an estimated two million bicycles in the capital.

Other Publications:

THE TIME-LIFE ENCYCLOPAEDIA
   OF GARDENING
HUMAN BEHAVIOUR
THE ART OF SEWING
THE OLD WEST
THE WORLD'S WILD PLACES
THE EMERGENCE OF MAN
LIFE LIBRARY OF PHOTOGRAPHY
TIME-LIFE LIBRARY OF ART
FOODS OF THE WORLD
GREAT AGES OF MAN
LIFE SCIENCE LIBRARY
LIFE NATURE LIBRARY
YOUNG READERS LIBRARY

Contents

I

Alleys and Palaces

The Peking dawn is unlike any other I have seen. At certain times of the year, most commonly in the spring, an almost imperceptible pall of fine dust lingers over the capital. It produces a quality of light, both grey and yellow, that is to be found only in this city and its surrounding Hopei province. The light is breathed as much as seen, and its effects are oddly equivocal; objects suddenly blur or sharpen, as though some superhuman finger were tampering with the focus. Whenever I think of Peking, I remember this mesmerizing phenomenon. The city and its first morning light seem perfectly attuned—at once unique, at once hazy and sharp, suggestive of a new beginning.

It may sound strange to liken so venerable a place to the dawn. After all, the first of many cities to rise on the site of Peking probably began forming in the Eighth Century B.C., at about the time of the legendary founding of Rome. In terms of historical attractions, Peking remains deeply fascinating. Among the surviving wonders of its past are the Great Wall of China—begun more than 2,000 years ago and still the only man-made structure on earth that is visible to the naked eyes of astronauts in outer space—and the Forbidden City, a central, 250-acre complex where feudal emperors isolated themselves in ultra-extravagant courts. Yet Peking derives little spiritual sustenance from its ancient roots. In a sense, this is a city at the dawn of its history, for Peking effectively turned its back on the past in 1949, when the Communists chose it as the capital of the People's Republic of China.

Since then, the city has experienced the most dramatic metamorphosis imaginable, changing more rapidly and profoundly than any other capital city on earth. In 1949 it had a population of roughly two million, but it lacked major industries and had lost its status as the seat of government to the larger and more southerly city of Nanking a quarter of a century earlier. In today's China, Peking is second only to Shanghai in size and population: its main built-up area and suburban farms hold more than seven million inhabitants. As an industrial city, Peking ranks fifth in China, boasting enormous steel, petrochemical and textile plants, plus many hundreds of smaller factories.

The quality of life has undergone equally momentous alterations. In 1949, by the most conservative estimates, a quarter of Peking's population was suffering from malnutrition. The greater part of the city was scarred by slum conditions and, amid the grinding poverty, stood a mass of brothels, opium dens, gaming houses and seedy taverns. Today no one

A huge portrait of Mao Tse-tung, mounted on the Gate of Heavenly Peace in central Peking, seems to monitor a gentle snowfall. From the balcony of this 15th-Century portal, Mao proclaimed the founding of the People's Republic of China in October, 1949.

Ch'ang An avenue, the main east-west axis of central Peking, follows the wall of the old Imperial City towards huge state buildings modelled on Soviet styles.

need starve in Peking. Plenty of near-slum housing remains, but there are virtually no beggars or prostitutes and almost certainly no drug-pedlars on the streets, and I personally do not know of a single bordello or gaming house in town.

This absence of vice in itself makes Peking an unusual 20th-Century city. More extraordinary, it is a city without privately owned cars, without churches (excluding two relics, one Catholic and one Protestant), without commercial advertising, and without any night-life (even most restaurants are closed by 8.30 p.m.). It is also a city where few birds sing, and flies rarely fly. Why? Because they have no place in the essentially new order of things. In the 1950s, the germ-carrying fly suffered a terrible blow when a government campaign exhorted the people of China—about 600 million at the time—to make a point of swatting 10 flies each and every day. The government also decided that birds had been consuming too much grain from the fields. A decree went out, and the entire population, working in relays, maintained a 24-hour din by blowing whistles and beating tin cans, trays and Chinese gongs. In fright, millions upon millions of birds took wing and remained in the air until they dropped dead from heart failure. Most of the birds now seen in Peking are caged canaries or other avian pets.

The ability of the authorities to mobilize most of the populace into working for a common purpose explains how Peking, along with the rest of China, has managed to change more in a few decades than it had done during the preceding 500 years of imperial rule. It should be added, however, that the people of Peking are not always the paragons of obedience, energy and co-ordinated dedication that the government would have the world believe them to be. I have seen workers idling on building sites and in factories in a way that would hardly be tolerated even in Britain; and I know of strikes, go-slows and brawls that have disrupted Chinese factories for months on end.

However, it is not my purpose here to make a political analysis of life in Peking or to weigh up the merits and demerits of the Communist system. Principally, my aim is to describe the city itself and how it feels to live in the middle of China today, in the heart of a capital that exemplifies a new way of life for some 900 million people.

Geographically, Peking occupies roughly the same position in China as does New York in North America—both verging on the 40th Parallel, both having their most comfortable temperatures in autumn and spring. But there all similarity ends. Located on the edge of the North China Plain, Peking is essentially a huddled city, sheltering behind hills and mountains to its north and west, and gazing proudly but a shade wistfully towards the warm and fertile lands of southern China. It stands neither on a significant river nor beside the sea. The nearest port is Tientsin, which lies about 70 miles away to the south-east.

The choice of this remote and relatively infertile spot as a city-site was perfectly logical in terms of China's needs some 27 centuries ago. The ancestor-city of Peking was built as a frontier outpost—a garrison to guard the North China Plain against marauding barbarian tribes, which could attack only via the Nan-k'ou and Ku-pei-k'ou passes in the Mongolian mountains to the north. The city was able to win a larger status only through centuries of beehive labours against its natural handicaps. Beginning in the Seventh Century B.C., great irrigation schemes transformed the dusty North China Plain into a creditable agricultural region; in the Seventh Century A.D., a 1,000-mile canal was dug to link the city with the rice-bowl of the Yangtze Valley to the south; in the 20th Century communications were further improved by the construction of an extensive railroad network, with Peking as China's principal northern junction.

Only one natural handicap has sternly defied all Chinese ingenuity and endeavour. That is the capital's unfortunate climate: oppressive in summer, frigid in winter, with too short an autumn and spring, and too much dust for a large part of the year.

The winter lasts a full five months—from the beginning of November until the end of March. Although Peking enjoys a clear blue sky on most winter days, temperatures frequently drop below 20°F.—and sometimes well below zero. Some of the new apartment blocks have central heating, but most dwellings are still warmed by old-fashioned iron stoves, sparingly fuelled with rolled-up balls made by mixing anthracite dust and tar. Household temperatures hover at a level that Westerners would find intolerably cold and outer clothing is very often worn in the house.

During one of the duststorms that strike Peking in winter and spring, a haze of soil particles blown in from the Gobi Desert envelops factories on the city's outskirts. At right, soldiers sweep up the layer of grit dropped outside their barracks by the north-westerly winds.

Throughout the winter months, a huge proportion of the population suffers visibly from colds, coughs and influenza.

There is virtually no rain in winter, and very little snow. If and when snow falls, it is welcome in the surrounding countryside because it means moisture for the early summer wheat crops and the rice and sorghum fields. But in the city it is detested as an impediment to bicycles—the chief means of personal transport in Peking. Armies of citizens sweep up the snow so fast that hardly a bicycle tyre or boot has time to mark its tread.

At times the dry winter cold is invigorating, the scene idyllic. Ice sheaths the trees. Lakes and moats become playgrounds for tens of thousands of children; bundled up in heavily padded clothes and mufflers, they cavort about on skates or on home-made ski-boards, which they propel from a squatting position with two short sticks. Mostly, however, the season is made thoroughly uncomfortable by freezing blasts sweeping down from Mongolia. From a foreigner's roomy, central-heated apartment, it is easy to tell which way the wind is blowing—by watching the Chinese cyclists, who are either free-wheeling at a merry pace or, heads down and dismounted, pushing their bikes against the lung-freezing gusts. Even without this clue, you can safely bet that the wind is blowing from the north-west.

Spring—the briefest of seasons in Peking—arrives in early April, when the poplar trees suddenly sprout long, furry-looking excrescences that drop to the street and are promptly swept up. The change brings welcome relief from the cold, but it also brings a new menace: a deluge of dust—actually fine soil from the Gobi Desert and from the suburban communes, where much of the food of Peking is produced. When high winds

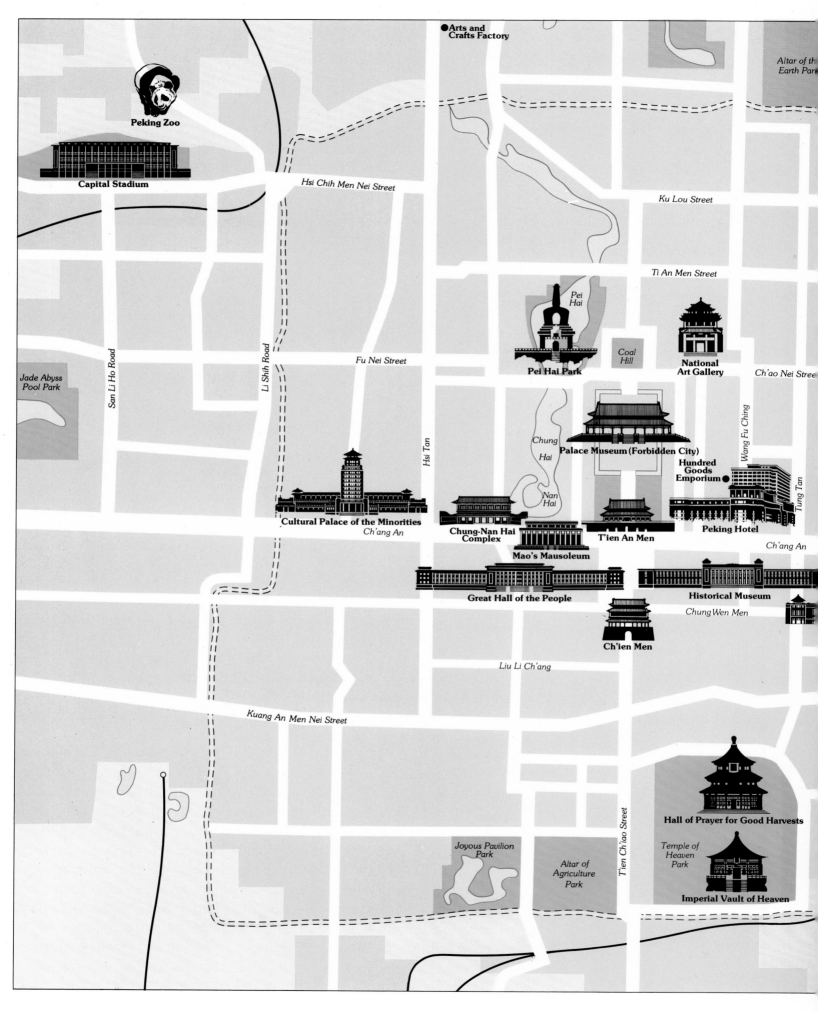

●Arts and Crafts Factory

Altar of the Earth Park

Peking Zoo

Capital Stadium

Hsi Chih Men Nei Street

Ku Lou Street

Ti An Men Street

San Li Ho Road

Li Shih Road

Fu Nei Street

Pei Hai

Coal Hill

Pei Hai Park

National Art Gallery

Ch'ao Nei Street

Jade Abyss Pool Park

Hsi Tan

Chung Hai

Wang Fu Ching

Palace Museum (Forbidden City)

Hundred Goods Emporium ●

Cultural Palace of the Minorities

Ch'ang An

Nan Hai

Chung-Nan Hai Complex

Tung Tan

Mao's Mausoleum

T'ien An Men

Peking Hotel

Ch'ang An

Great Hall of the People

Historical Museum

Chung Wen Men

Ch'ien Men

Liu Li Ch'ang

Kuang An Men Nei Street

T'ien Ch'iao Street

Hall of Prayer for Good Harvests

Joyous Pavilion Park

Altar of Agriculture Park

Temple of Heaven Park

Imperial Vault of Heaven

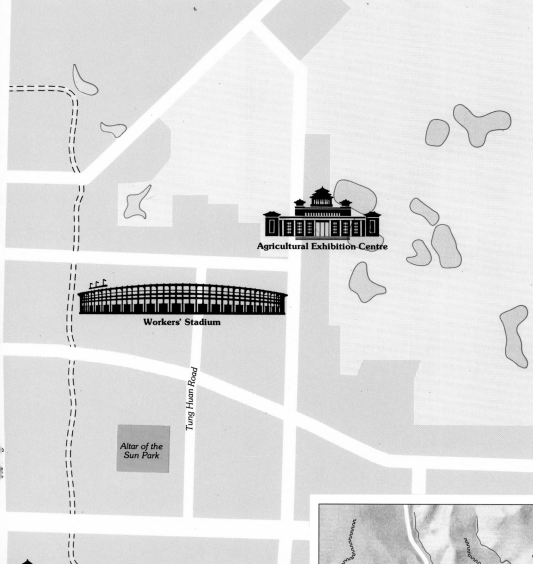

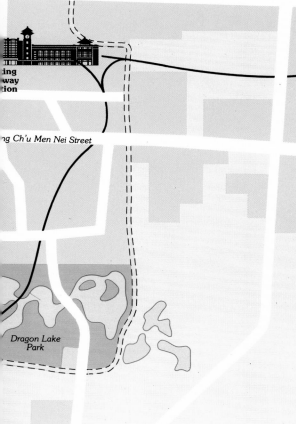

Agricultural Exhibition Centre

Workers' Stadium

Tung Huan Road

Altar of the Sun Park

ing
way
tion

ing Ch'u Men Nei Street

Dragon Lake Park

A Compass-planned City

Although much has changed in Peking since the Communist takeover in 1949, the city still retains the grid plan—oriented according to the cardinal points of the compass—given to it in the 15th Century. At that time, a pattern of straight avenues was laid out around the central palace complex that became known as the Forbidden City. A walled belt of fortifications (dotted black line on the map at left) marked the perimeter of the capital, then about 26 square miles in area.

The Forbidden City lost its focal importance, along with its imperial residents, after the republican revolution of 1911, and has since become the Palace Museum. The walls of Peking have been demolished, and the built-up area (shaded pink on the large map) stretches far beyond its old limits in a sprawl of industrial developments and suburbs.

In spite of its rapid growth, urban Peking accounts for only a fraction of the territory that now bears the city's name. By an administrative decision of 1959, Peking's boundaries have been extended to cover a 6,600-square-mile municipality (outlined in red on the inset map) that includes satellite towns and agricultural communes as well as such tourist attractions as the Ming Tombs and a much-visited section of the Great Wall.

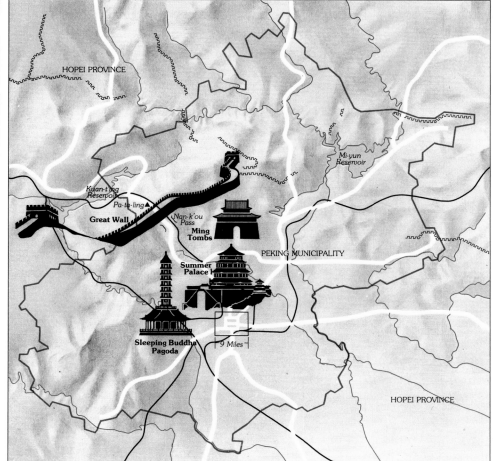

HOPEI PROVINCE

Mi-yun Reservoir

Kuan-t'ing Reservoir

Pa-ta-ling ▲

Great Wall

Nan-k'ou Pass

Ming Tombs

PEKING MUNICIPALITY

Summer Palace

Sleeping Buddha Pagoda

9 Miles

HOPEI PROVINCE

blow, watch out. The fine carpet of yellow powder covering Peking is churned into howling sandstorms that choke the city, flay the skin, mat the hair, and penetrate everywhere—through windows, doors, clothing and into books and papers. During these storms the inelegant style of Peking clothing is fully appreciated. The high-collared, quilted tunics and the baggy trousers (sometimes tied with string at the ankles) are an excellent defence against dust as well as cold. Many people gain further protection by wearing padded white surgical masks, taped around the ears.

A flush of yellow and pink on the parkland shrubs announces the arrival of springtime proper. The city authorities send out workmen to water the roots of trees that have been planted by the millions to serve as windbreaks and to provide shade in the summertime. Unfortunately, most of these trees are deciduous—ash, willow and poplar—and in winter they give hardly any protection against wind-blown dust. Moreover, as soon as they reach a worthwhile size, they are chopped down for valuable timber and replaced with fresh saplings.

The summer lasts from May until September. It is the only time of the year when any appreciable amount of rain falls; and it moistens the soil enough—with supplementary water from reservoirs and artesian wells— to permit the planting of a second grain crop for autumn reaping. Between June and August, however, the climate is uncomfortably hot and humid. Much of the populace seeks relief outdoors—sitting on walls and door-steps, hiring rowing-boats on the artificial lakes that were once reserved for the Imperial court, and lazing in the parks.

Autumn in the Peking parks is not like autumn in any ordinary wooded place. Here, one may never enjoy wading ankle-deep in a sea of rust-coloured leaves. The fallen leaves—like everything else—are swept up almost as soon as they touch the ground. Even small children go around picking them up, one by one, using pointed sticks. The foliage is not wasted. Any dry organic matter is useful as fuel and kindling, both for warmth and for cooking; and certain kinds of leaves may be fermented to make fertilizer or hog-feed for the communes. Peking's miracle-workers cannot control the weather, but they do their utmost to turn it to advantage.

I came to Peking for the first time in autumn. It was 1972, shortly after Richard Nixon broke down the insular policies that had barred most Westerners from China since the 1949 revolution. In the wake of President Nixon's visit, foreign governments fell over each other to with-draw recognition from Taiwan and extend it to Peking. Diplomats, journalists, language teachers, translators and airline representatives began to arrive in the city in droves. My mission was to open a bureau for *The Times* of London. China had always intrigued me. As a boy I had developed an interest in Chinese poetry; and at Cambridge University in the early 1960s, I studied Chinese language, literature and history.

Against a backdrop of dilapidated, identical huts, ice-cutters working on the frozen moat around the Forbidden City manoeuvre square floes towards the bank.

At the moat's edge, the floes are cut into blocks and dispatched to storage cellars. The ice will be used during the summer to refrigerate perishable foods.

Peking remained my professional and personal stamping ground for the next three-and-a-half years. After a spell of that length in Peking, one is regarded by most other foreigners as being almost a veteran resident; only a few score devotees of the Chinese Communist system stay on as foreign residents for more than four years. Most of the others are rotated to other postings by their employers or leave of their own free will, feeling that they have learned as much about China as that circumspect country is prepared to allow them to.

Peking does not yield itself readily to the new observer. Its subtle beauty and character are unobtrusive, and the city unfolds itself by way of a confusion of hazy and totally strange images that slowly merge to shape something less than a clearly defined picture. I remember my first long look at Peking as an anticlimax. From my sixth-floor apartment about two miles from the metropolitan centre, I gazed out on to a cityscape that was flat, rectangular and frankly monotonous. My abiding impression was of one enormous rabbit-warren: acre upon acre of labyrinthine *hu-t'ung* (alleyways) flanked by a confusion of interlocking courtyards. Not exactly what Marco Polo had led one to expect. When that 13th-Century Venetian globe-trotter feasted his eyes on Kublai Khan's Peking (then called Ta-tu, meaning Great Capital), he was inspired to write about a city with "the greatest and most wonderful palaces that were ever seen".

Modern Peking does not lend itself to superlatives; indeed, any architectural judgment tends to be tinged by regret. The array of ceremonial gateways and towering boundary walls that Marco Polo saw has almost completely disappeared—a sad but perhaps necessary sacrifice to re-development schemes. Those schemes have introduced much banal architecture to central Peking: modern apartment blocks and administration buildings of starkly utilitarian design. And in suburbs to the south and especially to the east, the enormous industrial growth is marked by wide-ranging chimney stacks belching smoke into the dust-filled air.

Most foreign residents are required to live and work in high-rise compounds located mostly in eastern and north-eastern Peking. These compounds are modern in style and extremely luxurious by local standards, but they are prone to such ills as falling masonry, recalcitrant elevators and malfunctioning drains. When I arrived, the construction of the apartment blocks was in full swing and pile drivers, manned by military construction crews, thumped through the night under blazing lights. A Greek diplomat, infuriated by the noise, temporarily disrupted the proceedings one night by parking his car across the entrance to a construction site in order to block trucks—a deed whose audacity astounded the workers. Having made his point, he consented to remove his car and return to bed—whereupon the din of construction resumed.

The most serious drawback to these compounds is their isolation from the everyday affairs of the city. All Chinese are prevented from entering

With his personal means of transport kept close at hand, a white-jacketed policeman directs traffic on Ch'ang An avenue. Although Peking has no private cars, the main thoroughfares are crowded with buses, lorries and military vehicles, and in narrow streets the authorities sometimes have to put up signs (right) that ban just about everything except bicycles.

the foreigners' quarters unless they have a special pass. If you met a Chinese in a park and tried to bring him home for tea, not only would he be stopped by the uniformed soldier at the gate, but there would be an extensive investigation into his motives and background.

Outside the compounds, foreigners are continually frustrated in their efforts to penetrate the life of the people. They are encouraged by officialdom to use stores and shops catering exclusively to the non-Chinese and they are steered to restaurants that have specially secluded rooms for alien patrons. The attitude of the authorities is that foreigners should be treated as privileged but suspect visitors—housed, fed and chauffeured in a style completely denied to the ordinary citizens of Peking. Foreigners who venture to regular shops are usually served ahead of other customers; and in restaurants lacking secluded rooms, they will often be given tables to themselves, even if it means reshuffling Chinese patrons. Again and again, the outsiders come up against a wall of courtesy combined with control; and eventually it drives many of them, psychologically and physically, back into their compounds—back to their more familiar life of cocktail parties, swimming, tennis, paper-pushing, politics, gossip and adultery.

For those newcomers who are determined to get to know the city, the most logical course of action is to import a car or borrow a bicycle—but this approach presents its own hazards and frustrations. Who would imagine that a city without any private cars could be as confusing as any other great metropolis during the rush-hour? Yet such is the case: for most of the daylight hours, central Peking is a nightmarish vortex of bicycles, pedicabs, three-wheeled vans, red trolley buses, lorries, Toyota taxis, and the occasional Shanghai limousines and old Russian-built Volga cars carrying Party or government officials on some unknowable business. Driving or cycling through the city is like swimming in a river full of bobbing, floating objects—all of unpredictable behaviour. Cyclists blatantly ignore traffic lights. Pedestrians jay-walk recklessly. And the majority of drivers seem to have no conception of practicable speeds.

The Chinese philosophy of traffic control is fundamentally a humane one. It purports that self-powered human beings are the ultimate owners of the road and that the onus is on motor-powered beings to take exceptional care not to strike those on bicycles or on foot. The traffic code bans drivers from eating, smoking or talking while driving—though not, astonishingly, from drinking! And every driver in Peking, male or female, observes to excess the chief rule of the road: *Honk!* Chinese drivers also have some curious techniques. Many of them start off in second gear on the flat and shift into top gear just as soon as the engine stops shuddering; very often they will cut the ignition long before reaching a red light and then free-wheel to a halt. In both cases, presumably, they imagine that they are conserving fuel.

Making the most of the daylight before work begins, a young man puts in some trumpet practice in a park near the centre of Peking. The mirror positioned on the tree branch allows him to check his lip-movements as he plays.

The traffic police—sitting or standing in booths at intersections—energetically direct the flow with red-and-white batons. But as often as not they add to the confusion. They lecture pedestrians incomprehensibly over loudhailer systems and they flick traffic lights on and off, sometimes changing their minds after a second or two. For no discernible reason, they may simultaneously turn on the "Stop", "Go", and "Caution" lights —and woe betide the driver who gets his mental wires crossed and fails to understand the policeman's intentions; he is liable to be subjected to a chewing-out such as the toughest New York traffic cop might admire.

Why does such chaos persist? Partly because the principle of lane-discipline has never been effectively introduced. But the chief problem seems to be the element of indiscipline in the Chinese political system itself. Instead of docilely submitting to a rebuke for having nearly caused an accident at an intersection, a Chinese cyclist may simply laugh and ride on; or he may suddenly turn red in the face with rage and bawl the policeman out for not "respecting the masses". On one occasion, I saw a uniformed soldier being forcibly restrained by a comrade from assaulting an on-duty traffic cop who had somehow offended him.

Lack of respect for the law can induce in the police a kind of controlled hysteria which, I am told by a Chinese friend, derives from the traditional Chinese notion that a display of public authority is ineffective unless accompanied by a show of anger. But displays of anger by the police

Morning Rituals

Peking springs to life in the morning with a ready energy that has no parallel among other great cities. Appropriately, matinal vigour is at its most impressive among the legions of physical-fitness devotees. During the hours between dawn and the start of work at 8 a.m., they swarm into the parks and open spaces, where they keep in trim by jogging or by practising one of the many types of *wu shu* (war arts) that have develop-ed in China over the millennia. Some of these arts require strenuous training routines with swords, spears and cudgels; but the most popular of all is a weaponless form of callisthenics known as *t'ai chi ch'üan* (ultimate supreme boxing). This stylized sequence of gestures—whose 128 basic movements take about 15 minutes to perform—evolved as a combat discipline; however, it now seems closer in spirit to ballet.

Elderly members of a t'ai chi ch'üan group go through their paces on open ground near the city centre.

In early sunlight, an athletic sexagenarian performs a routine imitating monkey postures—one of several forms of wu shu based on animal movements.

Soldiers jog across the 98-acre expanse of T'ien An Men Square. In the background is the Great Hall of the People, where major political gatherings are held.

seem to make no difference; they remain stymied in their attempts to impose order on busy highways. They tend to compensate by measures of petty discipline elsewhere: for example, by insisting that all cars parked outside a certain building should point in a perfectly straight line, with their front wheels aimed impeccably forward.

The spirit of free enterprise on the Peking highway may be all very fine for the bicycling millions, but it is no consolation to the foreigner anxious to remain a privileged guest of the Peking government. In a clash with officialdom, he can hardly expect the common crowd to rally round in support. My wife and I therefore employed a driver for our everyday transportation. However, we indulged in self-motoring in the first hours of daylight, and during the evenings or at weekends. Largely by way of "dawn patrols", cruising around in our small Japanese automobile, I familiarized myself with all of central Peking.

During the first hour of daylight, Peking is a motorist's dream. The main boulevards are broad and empty, some of them straight for miles on end, some curving gently left or right to disclose sudden vistas of ancient buildings and modern monuments. There is no need to keep alert, beyond watching out for the random cyclist who is pedalling home from his factory night-shift and who may swing dreamily across the road without troubling to look behind. And there is no real need to observe the city speed limits —normally about 30 m.p.h. on main highways and (in theory) 10 m.p.h. at busy road junctions. In these favourable conditions, let us make a short introductory tour of this most elusive of cities.

Less than a minute after leaving my eastern compound around 5.45 a.m., I am on Ch'ang An Ta Chieh (Avenue of Perpetual Peace), the main east-west artery running straight through the heart of the capital. Directly behind, the sun is just beginning to peep over the skyline of industrial suburbs; ahead, as far as the eye can see, the avenue—wider than the Champs-Elysées—stretches out like a deserted airport runway.

Near the heart of the city, I pull up at the tallest building on Ch'ang An: the Peking Hotel, a 17-storey edifice of which the civic authorities are inordinately proud. By Chinese standards, it is positively opulent. The immense lobby is dominated by a big wall-map showing the international time-zones; all rooms are fitted with electrically operated window curtains; thick-padded carpeting is laid throughout. At the front desk stand a few attendants in lumpy white uniforms. Otherwise, the lobby and corridors are deserted and I feel absurdly privileged at being able to operate the only fully automatic public elevators in all Peking.

My reason for calling at the Peking Hotel is to enjoy one of the best overviews of the city. Looking out from this central crow's nest, one begins to understand more fully Marco Polo's description of the old Peking: "The streets are so straight and wide that you can see right along from end to end and from one gate to another," he wrote. "The whole city is arranged like a chessboard." The rectilinear symmetry of Peking's design is still very striking, in spite of the many violent upheavals that have occurred since Marco Polo's day. Influenced by geomancy and astrology, the Chinese have always displayed exceptional regard for the cardinal points of the compass. Nowadays, modern boulevards bisect such venerable north-south highways as Hsi Tan and Tung Tan and, as a result, Peking has developed a grid system of thoroughfares—like Manhattan's, but less rigid and with far fewer intersections. As in New York, a Peking driver does not talk about going left or right. He turns east, west, north and south (the Chinese also speak of lifting the east side of a piece of furniture or hanging up a coat on the west side of another).

From the hotel, one can see clearly how the city was originally arranged, with absolute precision, on a north-south axis (see map, pages 10-11). The axis passes directly through Ch'ien Men (Front Gate), the main portal between the former Outer and Inner Cities; it proceeds thence through T'ien An Men (Gate of Heavenly Peace), the southern entrance to the former Imperial City; and it follows on to Wu Men (Meridian Gate), at the threshold of the Forbidden City.

Forbidden City and Imperial City? Inner City and Outer City? Like Chinese box-puzzles, Peking's cities within cities can be bewildering and demand some explanation. Quite simply, while Peking was aligned along the cardinal points of the compass, it was also planned in the form of concentric rectangles, each consisting of a walled enclosure. This was the design adopted by the Mongol ruler Kublai Khan when he rebuilt the city that his grandfather, Genghis Khan, had destroyed in 1215. It was also the design of the third Ming emperor, Yung-lo, who had the city dismantled and almost completely reconstructed between 1404 and 1421.

The capital of the Ming dynasty covered an area roughly three and a quarter miles long and four miles wide. This was Peking proper, otherwise called the Inner City. Within the Inner City was the Imperial City, a 1,500-acre pleasure-ground that was the exclusive preserve of the emperor's court. And within the Imperial City was the still more sacrosanct Forbidden City, an area normally barred to everyone except the emperor, his family and his most favoured concubines, eunuchs and guards. The adjoining Outer City was not part of the original Ming plan; as suburbs spread south from the Inner City in the 16th Century, emperors threw up a new set of walls enclosing an area of about 10 square miles. Today, these cities-within-cities are one, and they comprise about half of the main urban area of Peking.

In most capitals, a tour of the city at dawn serves no more useful purpose than to learn the layout of the streets and view the façades of lifeless buildings. In Peking it is different. On an excursion in the first hour of daylight, one learns much about the character as well as the structure of the city.

Having surveyed the city from above, we will now follow a simple rectangular course from the Peking Hotel—heading north on Wang Fu Ching avenue, then turning west to drive around the walled and moated perimeter of the old Forbidden City. It is a journey of no more than five miles; and yet, along the way, it unfolds all manner of impressions of the capital's extraordinary life-style.

First, Wang Fu Ching. As late as the 1930s, the street was a veritable carnival of charging rickshaws, vociferous pedlars, prostitutes, magicians, fortune-tellers and jugglers. Today it is a street of essentially utilitarian design, redeveloped as a formal shopping mall and including the concrete slab that is Peking's biggest department store, Pai Huo Ta Lou (Hundred Goods Emporium). The window displays are fairly unimaginative by Western standards and there is no trade-brand advertising—a reminder that this is a world totally lacking in competition among shopkeepers or manufacturers of similar goods. Yet many lamp-posts and walls (particularly near bus-stops) are plastered with such notices as "Engineer in Shenyang seeks similar in Peking to swap posts . . .", "Two-room apartment sought in eastern city in exchange for courtyard accommodation near Kuang An Men Railroad Terminal . . .". Aside from newspaper listings of movies and plays, these notices are the only form of private advertising permitted in Peking—and they, too, are carefully controlled. A person may change jobs or residences only after receiving the permission of the authorities, for every aspect of life in China is theoretically dictated by the Grand Design of the totalitarian state.

Although Peking may be strangely silent at sunrise, the city awakes with sudden vigour. What are the first signs of life after dawn? They may include a woman in a hygienic face-mask driving an electric dustcart that clears the gutters with rotating wire brushes, or perhaps the whisper of trolley buses picking up early-shift commuters. But most citizens of Peking do not have to report to factories, offices or schools until 8 a.m., and they take advantage of the day's first light to engage in a public ritual that can only be described in the colloquialism, "doing their own thing". One might come across an old man airing his pet canary, or an opera singer throwing her voice against an ancient wall; and in the parks one is certain to see scores of people going through some of the 128 postures of *t'ai chi ch'üan* —a form of exercise, conducted either independently or in groups, that combines elements of ballet and shadow boxing.

Around 6.30 a.m., I turn left (or rather, west) off Wang Fu Ching and travel along the northern side of the Forbidden City—no longer forbidden but redesignated the Palace Museum. Here, the fascination of historic Peking asserts itself more and more. In Marco Polo's day, the parkland to the north and west of the Imperial palaces was filled with "white stags and fallow deer, gazelles and roebucks, and fine squirrels of various sorts". His descriptions of wildlife have not the slightest relevance today, but

On the eve of October 1 — China's National Day — festive lights trace the pagoda-shaped roof of T'ien An Men and the new 17-storey tower of the Peking Hotel.

woods, grassy knolls, scattered pagodas and sweeps of shining water combine to maintain the exquisite loveliness of the area.

Directly to our north is Prospect Hill, a great artificial mound one mile in circumference. Legend has it that an early Ming emperor hoarded supplies of coal at this spot, and today it is still popularly known as Coal Hill. Whether or not the legend has any truth, the hill was mostly formed with earth excavated in creating the Forbidden City's moat. It was a natural dumping ground, because a hill at this point would protect the Imperial palaces against evil spirits which, according to superstition, emanated from the north.

Continuing westwards, we draw near the pleasure gardens that Kublai Khan created around three artificial lakes named Pei Hai, Chung Hai and Nan Hai (North, Middle and South Lake respectively). Until the establishment of the Chinese Republic in 1912, the ordinary Chinese citizen was strictly denied the beauties of this so-called Three Seas area. And even today, the immediate vicinity of Chung Hai and Nan Hai remains a mystery —a restricted zone reserved for political leaders who enjoy absolute privacy in pavilion residences.

The closest we can get to the residential complex is the road bridge spanning Pei Hai at its southernmost point. The bridge is guarded by soldiers and so I park the car at the eastern side and approach on foot, swinging my camera with much show and making it absolutely clear in advance what I want to photograph. To take pictures of the landscaped park across the water to the north is all right. To point your camera south, in the direction of Chung Hai and Nan Hai may not be.

I do not want to give the impression that you have to be super-careful with a camera in Peking. No one with any common sense will try to take pictures of military objectives in a Communist country, but otherwise you are presumably allowed to photograph almost anything you can see, since there are no notices forbidding photography in specific places. At the same time, you can run up against unexpected taboos—such as the rear of the Chung Hai and Nan Hai pavilions—and then you are liable to have your film confiscated.

A friend of mine—an Australian diplomat—was once taking shots near this bridge when a plain-clothes Chinese security man grabbed his arm to make him desist. My friend demanded to see the man's identity card. The agent refused and just kept tugging his arm. With immortal presence of mind, the diplomat shouted in Chinese to the army sentry: "Liberation Soldier! Come to my aid! This fellow is assaulting me!" The security man melted away, the sentry looked embarrassed—and my friend had the sense to stop trying to take pictures.

At times, of course, one has an overwhelming temptation to snap someone doing something unmistakably Chinese, but you should not take photographs of ordinary people if they make it evident that they object. Failure to observe this common courtesy can lead to unpleasant incidents. This happened to me as I drove along the edge of Pei Hai Park one morning and saw several dozen adults going through the graceful motions of *t'ai chi ch'üan*. I swung the car round in a sharp U-turn, wound down the window and pulled up just in range to take a picture of the group. A shout of warning went up from one of them; and they all stopped their exercises and looked pointedly in the opposite direction. I drove off, feeling more stupid than annoyed.

It is wrong to interpret this kind of reaction as merely a sign of hostility to foreigners. Ordinary citizens of Peking—as opposed to those in authority—are by nature a fairly friendly, gregarious and unself-conscious people. They cherish personal relationships and love to go out in groups, whether for morning exercise sessions or picnics in the parks or excursions in the hills outside the city. But, contrary to the widespread belief that their individuality has been completely swallowed up in the interests of totalitarianism, they have their personal pride and, in their moments of leisure, they like to preserve their own private world. (Also, they do not want to be portrayed in foreign publications.)

Peking's early morning rush-hour is now upon us, and so I head back east along Ch'ang An towards our starting point, the Peking Hotel. The route takes us directly past the spiritual hub of all China: T'ien An Men, the vermilion-walled, yellow-roofed Gate of Heavenly Peace. Here, centuries ago, the emperors' officials knelt to receive imperial edicts that were wedged in the beak of a carved and gilded phoenix and were let down from the parapet above. And here, from that same parapet, on the afternoon of October 1, 1949, Mao Tse-tung formally proclaimed the establishment of the People's Republic of China.

T'ien An Men! The patriotic emotions stirred by that name are extraordinary; no city except Mecca or Moscow has a monument to match its magnetic hold on hundreds of millions of people. Enough to say, perhaps, that it is almost inconceivable that any citizen of the People's Republic would visit Peking for the first time without making a pilgrimage to this focal point of Chinese Communism. Moreover, many new visitors have themselves photographed standing on one of the little wooden platforms in T'ien An Men Square, with their backs to the great entrance gate. Half a dozen professional photographers with old-fashioned plate cameras are permanently on duty there. Except in the most inclement weather, each of them has a queue of Chinese tourists eager to be snapped in the place they hear or read about almost *every* day of their lives.

We have reached the focal point of the new Peking. During the Great Leap Forward in 1958 and 1959, when Mao Tse-tung drafted virtually the entire adult population to work full- or part-time on various national projects, T'ien An Men Square was expanded from 27 acres to 98 by clearing away residential buildings. Everything here is larger than life, but my overall impression is of a cultural and architectural jumble. North of the square, beyond the gate, are somewhat over-elaborate palaces dating back to the 15th Century. The west side is blocked off by the Graeco-Roman geometry of the Great Hall of the People, a columned edifice where the government meets and visiting dignitaries are entertained with sumptuous feasts. Its style is echoed by the façade of the Historical Museum to the east. At the centre of the square stands the 124-foot, obelisk-like Monument to the People's Heroes—now completely overshadowed by the towering mausoleum where Mao Tse-tung's body can be seen on display. And beyond the mausoleum, to the south, the square peters out in pines and other trees and some modest buildings of an indeterminate neo-baroque style.

One cannot fail to be impressed by a pot-pourri mixed on such a staggering scale. When I was working as *The Times* correspondent in Moscow before coming to China, I considered Red Square to be awesome. Peking's great square is many times larger, affording room for hundreds of thousands of people. The Great Hall and the Historical Museum are both a full quarter of a mile in length. The former has a marbled, chandeliered entrance hall 100 yards long and a banqueting hall that can comfortably seat several thousand guests for dinner. Government propaganda proudly asserts that both the Great Hall and the Historical Museum, together with eight other large buildings in the vicinity, were completed in 10 months of frantic endeavour—10 buildings in 10 months to mark the tenth anniversary (in the tenth month of 1959) of the founding of the People's Republic of China.

I believe that the people of Peking may now have reason to regret this burst of frenetic energy, since the buildings—inspired by Soviet architecture—are quite out of harmony with the city's past or its future. Such edifices are already considered quaint in Moscow, and in Peking they are downright incongruous—a cultural crime against the capital city of the world's oldest coherent civilization. When the Peking authorities get round to a thorough replanning of their city, instead of the stop-gap measures of recent years, let us hope that the bulldozers start on the buildings here, at the symbolic centre of polity for almost a quarter of mankind.

Muscle-powered Traffic

Ignoring its master's cajolery, an ill-behaved donkey—being trained for future transport duty—pits its weight against the horses at the head of a cart.

Like other modern metropolises, Peking keeps its commuters and commerce on the move with buses, trains and trucks—but mechanized transport is by no means the whole story. Since China's limited production of haulage vehicles is earmarked for factories or farms whose output ranks high on the list of state priorities, the city has to rely on muscle power for many bulk-carrying tasks. Donkeys, mules and horses pull rubber-tyred carts through the city streets; and humans, too, regularly put themselves in harness to haul modest-size loads. As for personal travel, only a comparative handful of officials, military personnel and other important personages have automobiles at their disposal. The bicycle—which costs about $70, or twice the average monthly wage—remains Peking's chief means of transportation and a worker's most fundamental possession.

A mountain of waste cardboard, topped by two sanitation workers, almost submerges the horse pulling the load to a plant where the strips will be recycled.

Blocks of ice, hacked from frozen lakes during the winter and stored in underground sawdust-lined pits, move towards shops and markets on a summer's day.

Teamsters plod alongside a snow-dusted caravan of carts transporting sacks of grain from an outlying commune's granary to a depot in the centre of Peking.

A worker hauls a barrowful of bricks to a construction project in north-east Peking. Bricks are usually fired in temporary kilns set up near building sites.

An Inexhaustible Energy Source

Much of the energy for transport in Peking comes from that most abundant of resources—
people. Agricultural communes within the city limits place an especially large claim on
human muscles for haulage; among the chief contributors are students, who must put in a
stint of rural labour each year. Elsewhere in the metropolis, pedal-power is an answer to
transport chores. Fortunately for a city so short on machines, Peking's terrain is mostly flat.

As part of their "lao-tung"—manual labour obligations—schoolboys drag a cartload of river weeds to a commune. It will be used for pig feed and fertilizer.

A band of students, clearing a building site of rubble and weeds during their "lao-tung", struggle to wrest their heavy-laden barrow out of a ditch.

A chair fitted with wheels serves an old man as a means of mobile support.

A genial retiree gives a youngster a ride in a wooden pram with room for two.

Secure in his father's sidecar, a red-capped youngster gazes at the scenery. Such bicycle auxiliaries are made at home or in neighbourhood workshops.

Two members of the People's Liberation Army convey sewage collected at public latrines to farms in the country, where it will later be converted into fertilizer.

In the absence of a system of motorized hearses, a volunteer—accompanied by a friend—transports a corpse to a crematorium on a specially adapted bicycle.

2

Life in a Lockstep Society

In 1969, when a touring team of Chinese athletes in Europe were given the news that America had landed the first men on the moon, their spokesman replied: "We will put the first new men on earth." This was not said in jest. Every Chinese political activist is expected to believe that his government is paving the way to the Communist millennium. For many Chinese, however, the past has a disconcerting way of making itself felt in a world committed to the future. Even in Peking, where thousands of workers have been rehoused in large new apartment blocks, huge numbers still live in decaying and crowded old buildings with only a courtyard stand-pipe for water and a public latrine on the street outside.

These aging accommodations line the hundreds of *hu-t'ung*, or alley-ways, of the city. Varying in width from mere pathways, in which it is virtually impossible to stretch out both arms at full length, to narrow streets, on which two automobiles barely have room to pass, the *hu-t'ung* are either muddy or dusty, according to the vagaries of the weather; and they offer much evidence of that most unpleasant Chinese habit—spitting in public. The tiny houses on them are mostly one-storey structures, recalling Imperial times when nothing taller was allowed, lest citizens on an upper level be able to look down upon the emperor if he passed by.

The typical *hu-t'ung* dwelling is built around a central courtyard, presenting only blank walls to the outside world. At one time the walls protected family privacy, but nowadays each house is occupied by several families, perhaps spanning two or three generations, and everyone shares the inner open space. Such neighbourhoods are overwhelmingly grey— grey walls, grey roof tiles, grey flagstones. There is only an occasional touch of colour: perhaps a huge sunflower peeping over the top of an outer wall, or some smaller pot-plants decorating the lattice-work exterior of a courtyard entrance.

To tour the *hu-t'ung* on a summer evening, when many people are out of doors, is to see the personal and informal face of Peking. A woman emerges from a courtyard and flings a bowl of washing-up water on to the dusty, unpaved alleyway. A tiny songbird whistles in its cage. An old man with long whiskers and an even longer pipe sits on his doorstep, following your passage expressionlessly. A girl, her long hair falling loosely down her back, hurries home from a visit to the local bath-house. A few youths lounge around, gossiping. And then comes the abrupt reminder that you are actually walking down a street: several cyclists suddenly appear, bowling along among the strollers and jangling the bells on their handle-

An elderly woman with tiny, deformed feet— once considered a mark of feminine beauty— hobbles painfully across a Peking avenue with a youth's assistance. The ancient custom of binding the feet of high-born young girls was officially banned in 1911, but it persisted in China until the Communists took power.

bars. When they have passed by, you find you must press against a wall to make way for a donkey-cart that is carrying fresh vegetables.

All the men you encounter wear baggy cotton or synthetic-fibre trousers of subdued hues and plain, open-necked shirts. The greatest concessions to variety are the modest floral or polka-dot patterns of the women's blouses. In the mid-1970s, the subsequently discredited widow of Mao Tse-tung, Chiang Ch'ing, encouraged a few brave spirits to follow her example and wear dresses; but the experiment never really took hold. Skirts are rarely worn, and then only in summer. It is unusual for them to rise above the knee. Only the very young are free from the taboo against sartorial ostentation: their shorts and dresses are all gaily coloured, and most of the girls have their hair tied in bright ribbons. The infants' padded pants have slits in the rear; no Chinese mother thinks anything of holding her child in a sitting position and letting him relieve himself wherever convenient.

The unique medley of sights and sounds is endless. The wall of every house sports a device I have seen only in Peking: a tin can suspended by wire on the outlet pipe of an anthracite-burning stove. Its purpose is to catch the droplets of tar produced by condensation as the anthracite smoke hits the cold, dry air of the Peking winter. Doubtless, the tar accumulated from all the *hu-t'ung* cans can be used again: according to the Chinese, "All waste is treasure". This includes even human waste, or "black gold", which is collected from the public latrines by "honey-bucket men". After treatment to destroy disease-carrying organisms, the sewage is used as fertilizer on the commune fields that surround the city.

Nothing is too humble to be totally discarded, which is one reason why the streets of Peking are so conspicuously clean, except for dots of sputum. Another reason is the fear of disease. In spite of the spitting and the infants who relieve themselves in the street, litter is regarded as a potent source of infection. There are nightly collections of refuse; and on hot, dusty days, municipal water-tankers are for ever spraying the streets (the drivers usually take great care to turn down the jets when they pass pedestrians, but occasionally an unwary passer-by can get a soaking).

Less comprehensible is the mass prejudice against grass. As soon as a few blades appear in the parks or on the verges of streets, they are ruthlessly pulled up. To me, this has always seemed unnecessary, un-aesthetic and conducive to dust and erosion. I can only guess that it is meant to reduce the breeding grounds for insects, which have been an increasing nuisance since the largely successful campaign against birds in the 1950s. Certainly, the dislike of insects is justified, for they may carry deadly diseases, including encephalitis—inflammation of the brain—which is still endemic in the Peking area.

It is at such basic levels that the Chinese capacity for organization and discipline is at its most impressive. What many Western observers find

Pedestrians and cyclists throng a dusty alleyway in the Ch'ien Men district—formerly one of the city's red-light areas. Since 1949, the Communists have greatly reduced prostitution by "re-educating" the women and helping them find alternative employment.

repugnant is the application of these same principles to *all* aspects of life. Foreigners are often amazed by the total acceptance of a system that directs and regiments every citizen from the cradle to the grave. Part of the explanation lies in China's history. For three millennia the country was ruled by successive autocracies, a conditioning experience that enables the present regime to consolidate its own authority without too much trouble.

History offers no precedent, however, for the rigid *social* discipline that characterizes life in modern China. Dr. Sun Yat-sen, whose anti-monarchist movement succeeded in toppling the Manchu dynasty in 1911, once despairingly described the Chinese people as "a tray of loose sands"—a reference to the chronically fragmented nature of Chinese society. In 1936 another distinguished Chinese observer, Lin Yutang, offered a more detailed diagnosis of the problem. "Chinese society," he wrote, "is cut up into little family units, inside which exists the greatest communistic co-operation, but between the units no real bond of unity exists, except the state. As China has stood practically alone and unchallenged, even this sense of state, or nationalism, has not been greatly developed. So family consciousness has taken the place of the social consciousness and national consciousness in the West."

The Communists in China have tried to solve this problem, not by eliminating the kinship feeling, but by vastly enlarging its focus. Much the same relationship that has traditionally existed between the wise parents and the obedient child now exists between the Communist leadership and the mass of the people. This helps to explain the extreme political docility of the Chinese when their leadership is stable and self-confident.

Washing hung out to dry in a courtyard shared by several families lends a note of colour to an otherwise grey maze of traditional homes in central Peking.

Conversely, it helps to explain the malaise, hysteria and even brutality that occasionally occur when the people sense some faltering or division in the leadership. Quite simply, they show the symptoms of distress or delinquency that a child often displays when its parents are in conflict.

The surrogate parents exercise their influence and authority through a dual committee system that operates at every level of social and economic activity. Each factory, for example, has a so-called revolutionary committee of worker-representatives to manage its day-to-day affairs, as well as a committee of Communist Party members to provide the correct ideological impetus. The linchpins of each committee are the cadres, politically reliable officials appointed to implement party and government directives. Thus, the individual worker is never far away from the voice—or the ear—of patriarchal authority.

There is one sight in Peking that instantly places modern Chinese society in historical perspective. It is that of an old woman hobbling along on tiny, crippled feet, perhaps no more than three inches long. Here is living testimony of a medieval horror that survived well into the 20th Century. Right up to the Communist takeover in 1949, there were still status-conscious families who practised the ancient custom of binding the female child's feet. The process began at the age of five, when the toes were bent under the sole and then tightly bound with cloth. Every two or three weeks thereafter, the foot would be forced into a shoe one-tenth of an inch smaller than the last; and this torture might continue for 15 years.

Far more than the Victorian ankle, the bound foot—or "golden lily" as Chinese poets preferred to call it—was regarded as an erotically tantalizing part of the female anatomy; and the smaller the foot, the more desirable the woman. The victims won additional praise for their obvious willingness to suffer and obey. No doubt, a further attraction for men was the fact that a woman thus hobbled could never stray far from home.

Thus, the old lady tottering down a Peking street epitomizes the servitude in which Chinese women were formerly held. Constrained by Confucian precepts to observe "three obediences"—to the father, to the husband, and then to the son—they lived in a world of arranged marriages, polygamy and concubinage; and they usually had minimal political and economic rights.

The first great step in eliminating this prejudice was the Marriage Law enacted on May Day, 1950. The law laid down a minimum marriage age of 18 for women and 20 for men, gave married women the right to retain their maiden names, conferred joint rights in the possession and management of family property, and made divorce as well as marriage dependent on mutual consent. Although the centuries-old belief in male superiority persists among many older people, and the best jobs are mostly still held by men, sexual equality is now generally accepted in principle at least.

In spite of the youthful minimum age prescribed by law, early marriage is strongly discouraged because it is likely to boost the birth rate. In rural areas, where tradition is most strongly entrenched, it is not unusual for couples to wed in their late teens or early twenties; but in Peking and other large metropolitan areas, the accepted conjugal age is not less than 25 for women and 27 for men.

By contrast with some other Communist countries, including the Soviet Union, divorce in China is severely frowned upon, and every effort is made to keep couples together. First, neighbourhood activists will try to act as conciliators. If this approach fails, the couple may be summoned before a mass meeting of neighbours and workmates at which anyone may offer criticism and advice. If the couple still insists on divorce, they will have to plead their case before a Municipal People's Court, where further efforts at conciliation will be made. Only in the very last resort will divorce be permitted, and the social record of whoever is judged to be the guilty party may bear an indelible stain.

I once profoundly shocked a middle-aged man in Peking by telling him about the West's increasingly casual attitude towards sex. "But what about the effects on the children, and the danger of venereal disease being spread?" he asked. To be frank, I could think only of replying that venereal disease was curable if caught early enough, and that many people believed sexual freedom to be more important than social stability. He found such an attitude utterly degenerate and distasteful.

In China, it is considered highly improper for teenage boys and girls to take any kind of erotic or romantic interest in the opposite sex, and certainly no ambitious young person thinks of choosing a life-mate before attending a university, or working for a few years in an office, a factory or commune. A young man may then approach a female of suitable age and ask if she is interested in "developing" a relationship. Alternatively, if someone is too shy or unappealing to attract a partner, workmates or relatives may set about arranging dates with likely candidates.

With promising contact established, the ensuing period is somewhat similar to a Victorian courtship, though less elaborate. On weekends, the couple may go for walks in the park, perhaps visit a cinema together, or be received by each other's families. Then, if the two young people wish to take their relationship further, they will probably consult the revolutionary committees at their places of work. The committees will examine their political attitudes, and the couple could well be told to think again if one of the partners is deemed to display less than the required degree of rectitude.

Once a couple has been given the go-ahead, the marriage formalities take about five minutes. The two simply fill out a licence in front of the district registrar and have witnesses sign it. The parents of the bride or groom may then invite a few friends and relatives home to share

Outside a school that was formerly the home of a wealthy merchant, two young devotees of table tennis face off across a "net" of bricks placed on a concrete playing surface. Such all-weather tables for Peking's favourite racquet sport are to be seen throughout the city.

peanuts and tea or liquor with the newly-weds. For most couples, the big problem then becomes finding a home. They may have to go on living in separate factory dormitories for years or, worse still, they may be assigned work tasks in different parts of the country, which would prevent them from seeing each other more than once or twice a year. Personal preferences are taken into account when tasks are assigned, for it is accepted that an unhappy worker is likely to be an inefficient worker; but the main emphasis is on persuading the individual that selfish considerations must give way to the wider needs of the community.

Once a couple does succeed in finding a place to settle down—perhaps in two *hu-t'ung* rooms shared with relatives; or, ideally in a small apartment of their own in one of the new industrial suburbs—they are considered eligible to have a child. Like most Asians, people in Peking see no point in marrying without having at least one child; and they show almost universal distaste and astonishment on learning that many married people in the West lead active sex lives without planning to bear children.

At the same time, China is currently faced with a population growth rate of about 15 million a year, and so the authorities do everything in their power to discourage families from having more than two children. Special teams visit factories, workshops and communes to propagate the gospel of family planning. A man and wife who have just had a first child are expected to wait several years before having a second, and any family exceeding this optimum may be denied further childcare benefits. Anyone betraying such blatant lack of "social-spiritedness" might also incur a form of social ostracism, something that only the most tough-minded people are prepared to face.

After 56 days' paid maternity leave, mothers invariably go back to work, for female labour is now vital to the Chinese economy. In Peking, women make up about half the total workforce in light industry. A significant proportion are employed in both engineering and construction; and many unskilled mothers are organized into neighbourhood workshops, where they perform simple jobs such as sewing or flashlight assembly. Large enterprises often have their own nurseries, kindergartens and breast-feeding rooms; and grandparents are only too delighted to lend a hand in looking after the children.

The system is by no means unpopular, since most women welcome the chance to escape from the domestic scene and earn money. Although the husband will often prepare the evening meal, sexual equality in China does not inevitably embrace the notion of the independent career woman, which means that the Peking housewife with a profession is still primarily responsible for running the home. The availability of canteen meals and the introduction of piped water and electricity have helped to ease the female burden; but labour-saving devices are few and there is still plenty of back-aching drudgery for the mother of the family.

Behind the Grey Façades

Although Peking is putting up new apartment blocks as fast as resources will allow, the one-storey *hu-t'ung* homes in the older sections of the city still provide living quarters for many thousands of workers. Each house, originally built for a single family, is today shared by several families who rent units of two or three rooms from the state for about three yuan ($1.60) a month.

Life behind the grey-brick façades is austere. The state supplies electricity, but not running water; a solitary tap in the courtyard serves as the only water source; and any occupant who wants a full-length soak must repair to the local public baths. The rooms themselves—such as the kitchen and bedroom seen here—tend to be minimally furnished and lack most of the household appliances that are considered basic in Western cities. But everything is generally kept in good repair and spotlessly clean—a marked contrast to conditions in the pre-revolution past, when filth and decay reigned, disease was rampant, and—in the words of a writer of the 1930s—the people suffered "a destitution worse than animals".

A vase of flowers on a lace table-cloth brings a bit of cheer to a bedroom in one of Peking's courtyard homes. The basin serves as sink and bath.

In a typical Peking kitchen, kettles rest on a pair of simple gas hobs that are the sole cooking devices. The kitchen window panes are made of rice paper.

Radiators and gas stoves are provided in the new apartment blocks, where kitchen facilities are often shared. However, in many of the older houses heating and cooking are done with stoves fuelled by coal-dust balls. Made from a mixture of mud and coal-dust, the balls are dangerous as well as dirty, for when Peking seals up its doors and windows against the winter cold there is quite a high risk of poisoning from the carbon monoxide fumes.

A Peking worker usually rises between 5 and 6 a.m., allowing time to carry out some of the basic household chores before the start of the morning shift. Breakfast, which many people like to take in the restaurants run by their local neighbourhood committees, tends to be a substantial if simple meal. Noodle soup, red beans or bean curd may be followed by steamed bread rolls, sometimes stuffed with sugar or bean jam. As for beverages, tea is expensive, and plain boiled water is the most common drink. Copious quantities are consumed throughout the day, so that the water boiler is as indispensable to the Peking worker as the coffee-dispenser or tea-trolley is to his American or European counterpart.

After breakfast comes the scramble to get to work by bicycle or public transport. Although some efforts are made to house workers reasonably close to their offices or factories, commuter journeys of an hour or more each way are not uncommon. Travelling should become easier as the Peking subway network, begun in 1965, is expanded; more than 12 years after work was started, however, there was only a single line of 16 miles serving 16 stations, and this closed down promptly at 7.30 each evening.

A normal work-shift in office or factory starts at 8 a.m. and continues until 11.30 a.m., when there is a break for lunch and rest. The lunch-hour is the focal point of the day for most people. "Have you eaten yet?" is the standard polite inquiry. If Peking people sometimes seem obsessed by food, it is not because they are seriously underfed, but because they can remember the times when they were. Less than half a century ago, hundreds of people starved to death in the streets of Peking every year, and as recently as the 1960s a series of disastrous crop failures led to severe food shortages. Another factor is the traditional Chinese belief that correct nutrition is essential to the balance between mind and body.

A typical canteen luncheon menu might include noodle soup, bread rolls, and dumplings stuffed with meat or vegetables. Pork and mutton are the most popular meats, but sometimes chicken is used as a filling, and, on rare occasions, fish substitutes for meat. Having risen early, the people of Peking like to get their lunch over as quickly as possible so that they can take a short siesta, or *hsiu-hsi*, before the afternoon shift gets under way at 1.30 or 2 o'clock. Work continues until about 5 p.m. With production quotas fulfilled for another day, most people gratefully head for home to join the rest of the family for the evening meal—typically comprising yet more noodles and stuffed dumplings.

As part of a campaign to encourage birth control, a poster at a Peking clinic stresses the domestic happiness of a family with two children—the recommended maximum. It also lauds an additional contribution to the national weal: the rifle-cleaning man of the family is a member of the militia—a volunteer defence force that can be activated in times of crisis.

At least twice a week, however, people may have to stay at work to attend an hour-long political study session, and anyone failing to turn up can expect to incur the ire of the activists on the revolutionary committee. These seminars often begin with unison reading of quotations by the late Mao Tse-tung or tributes to the new Chairman, Hua Kuo-feng, and may then lead on to ritual denunciations of the current roster of political villains, variously characterized by such names as "revisionists", "factionalists", "ultra-leftists", "right-wing deviationists", or "capitalist roaders". Occasionally, the lurid idiom of Chinese folklore is invoked—in which case the villains may be caricatured as "monsters", "ogres", "ghouls", "demons" and "devils".

As well as conducting study sessions, the activists have a host of other duties to perform, from devising slogans and wall posters to assessing the attitudes of workmates. Minor infractions of "socialist discipline", such as occasional unpunctuality, will elicit a private warning; but repeated misconduct is likely to be the subject of a debate by the whole workforce, and the individual concerned is expected to show the correct degree of contrition and may be required to engage in public self-criticism. His or her "sin" may amount to no more than personal untidiness, but in today's China the personal and the political are inseparably linked.

Odious as this system may seem to people in the West, it is rooted once again in the traditional Chinese approach to family relationships. Personal fulfilment, as well as social esteem, used to depend on how well an individual functioned as a member of the family group. These same aspirations now depend on how well an individual functions as a member of the wider social group—be it kindergarten class, factory work-force, or Party committee. This is not to imply that the system is any-where near as perfect as its apologists like to pretend; while it may reflect some of the virtues of family life, it also reflects many of the faults. The Party zealot can be every bit as tiresome as the interfering aunt. On balance, though, people do seem to have a fairly deep sense of involvement.

In terms of material rewards, the system is by no means as even-handed as is sometimes assumed. In fact, the greatest single fallacy about Peking is that it is the capital of an egalitarian society. It is true that the range of gross incomes is much narrower than in the West, but the difference in earnings and lifestyle between the upper and lower echelons of Chinese society is nonetheless enormous. High government officials and senior army personnel drive around Peking in curtained limousines and buy imported cigarettes at the International Club, a favourite haunt of the foreign diplomatic community, while an industrial worker pedals his bike an hour or more to work in bitter cold or sweltering heat, and smokes cheap cigarettes that would never find a buyer in a Western supermarket.

Before her fall from political grace in 1976, Mao's widow, Chiang Ch'ing, apparently lived like an empress. The former actress had her own

Thousands of Peking citizens, celebrating the international labour festival of May Day, stroll along a lavishly decorated avenue in Temple of Heaven Park.

Responding to the relative privacy of a parkland glade, a courting couple allow themselves a degree of intimacy rarely observed in a public place.

collection of early "bourgeois" films, starring such foreign celebrities as Greta Garbo and Charles Chaplin; and it is alleged that in the space of a single month she ordered two dozen tailor-made dresses. The American Sinologist, Professor Roxane Witke, who had a long series of interviews with Madame Chiang during 1972, has described how a bodyguard once suddenly appeared bearing a large oblong box: "Laughing like a girl," the most powerful woman in China, as she was then, "lifted the cover and pulled out, as if by magic, one long pleated black skirt after another. 'I like skirts,' she announced as she handed out one each to her female attendants (myself excluded). 'And they're comfortable in summer.' I asked where they came from. 'From the Friendship Store!' No matter to her that the official line on the Friendship Stores was that they are reserved exclusively for foreign consumers."

The ordinary Peking family has rather less scope for spending sprees. In recent years, there have been eight basic wage grades for industrial workers, ranging from around 35 yuan per month (roughly $18) for apprentices to 110 yuan ($58) for skilled veterans. The average factory wage in Peking is 60 to 70 yuan per month; and even though the government imposes strict rent and price controls, few people can afford to buy more than the bare essentials. Certainly, the Chinese worker is better off now than he has ever been—but that is also the case with Western workers. In China, however, real wages have stagnated; the authorities are always eager to point out that there is no inflation in China, but that may be small comfort to people whose living standards remain at the same low level year after year.

Although workers get only one day off a week, those living away from home may be entitled to two weeks of paid annual vacation, which enables them to visit their families. There are also seven days of national holidays: January 1 and May 1; the anniversary of the founding of the People's Republic on October 1 (two days off); and the Chinese New Year, which is based on the old lunar calendar and falls during either January or February (three days).

The May and October holidays are given over to mammoth demonstrations of political solidarity. Even vegetables have a political role to play. Assistants at the city's shops and markets arrange their produce to spell out the characters for "May 1" or "October 1" and often show great reluctance to sell certain items for fear of spoiling their displays.

Although almost everyone is out in the streets during demonstration time, burglars appear to be about as rare as private entrepreneurs. The Chinese authorities are obsessively secretive about such matters, but it does seem—in Peking, at least—that the incidence of crime is minimal. I suspect that this is not entirely unrelated to the fact that anyone mysteriously acquiring a new bicycle, radio or sewing-machine would

The Peking Railway Station (centre), completed in 1959, rises amid old-style houses, new apartment blocks and factories located south-east of the city.

very soon come under scrutiny by the local street committee, which serves as the basic unit of urban administration.

Unlike the two political holidays, the Chinese New Year, or Spring Festival as it is now called, is essentially a family occasion. The shops are crowded with people queueing to buy sweets and toys for their children and small gifts for relatives and friends. Huge queues also form at the Peking Railway Station, since many people take the opportunity to visit relatives in remote parts of the country; even in temperatures well below freezing, one will see travellers lined up at the ticket offices or slumped on their bedrolls waiting for trains. Elsewhere in the city, groups of young people wander excitedly through the streets at night carrying paper lanterns and the daylight hours reverberate with the sound of exploding fire-crackers. The high point of the holiday occurs when thousands of youngsters run a marathon circuit of the Forbidden City. Although not specifically connected with the Spring Festival, the race usually takes place then because young people are encouraged to take winter exercise.

After the holiday, it's back to work. And for those who ultimately find their drab routine unacceptable, a short leave of absence can often be arranged without too much difficulty. Some people seem to attend their father's "funeral" several times over the years, and the smallest ailment suffered by oneself or a close relative will almost certainly merit a few days off. The fact that the Chinese are the world's champion hypochondriacs must be only too evident to Peking's overworked doctors, yet they willingly sign "rest" chits for minor or non-existent illnesses, apparently believing that prevention is better than cure.

Although most workers are covered by some form of medical insurance, a sick person and his family may still have to shoulder part of the financial burden—not least of which is the loss of earnings by someone suffering a long illness. Moreover, skilled medical attention is not always easy to obtain. In rural areas, people often have to rely on the services of "barefoot doctors"—medical auxiliaries who have received only three months of formal medical training. In large cities, such as Peking, a seriously ill patient may have to wait many weeks before a bed becomes available in one of the overcrowded hospitals. However, for all its short-comings, the system is a great advance over the past, when thousands died for lack of any kind of medical attention.

Over the past few years there has been renewed interest in traditional Chinese healing therapies, particularly acupuncture. Involving the in-sertion of needles into various specific points of the body, acupuncture has been widely and successfully used in the treatment of many conditions, including migraine headaches, rheumatism, appendicitis, diabetes, tuber-culosis and polio. In the late 1960s it was found that acupuncture tech-niques could remove all feeling of pain in related parts of the body for up to nine hours. As a result, Chinese surgeons have been able to carry out

During their lunch break, railway hands cluster on a platform at Peking's main station to play or watch Chinese chess, a game that utilizes checker-like pieces. Many of Peking's workers prefer to catnap after their midday meal.

long and complicated operations without needing to rely on conventional anaesthesia techniques, an approach to surgery that is not only cheaper but is also said to hasten the patient's recovery. Although, as yet, there is no scientific explanation for the remarkable effects of acupuncture, recent findings suggest that it stimulates chemical changes in the brain, and it is possible that these changes are an essential part of the healing process.

Improved hygiene, sanitation and medical services have all helped to raise average life expectancy far beyond its pre-1949 level. This gain means that most Chinese can now look forward to retirement—normally at the age of 55 for women and 60 for men. When retirement day finally arrives, the elderly worker may be ceremoniously hoisted on to the back of a small truck and paraded slowly down the street while workmates bang drums and cymbals to attract the attention of passers-by. Retired people are generally expected to remain active in the community, perhaps by looking after the children of working parents, by helping out with a neighbour's shopping, or by attending political meetings and describing what life was like in "the bitter past".

Married couples often live with their parents, but for the aged without family there are "Homes of Respect for the Elderly", where inmates are encouraged to perform simple tasks such as assembling light industrial products or tending a vegetable garden. Life in these homes is not nearly as grim as it may sound, for many residents like to prove that they are still capable of doing useful work. The staff try to create a family atmosphere by arranging for neighbourhood children to make frequent visits. At Spring Festival the authorities will usually provide funds so that the old folk can buy presents for these "adopted" grandchildren.

In the past, many elderly people sought comfort in religion, but most of the aged now seem to be as indifferent as the young. No one is permitted to visit Peking's Lama temple, and almost the only worshippers at the city's single mosque are diplomats from Muslim countries. Peking's two remaining churches—one Catholic and one Protestant—fare no better. A few elderly Chinese make an occasional appearance there, and Chinese choirs sing at Christmas and Easter; but the congregations consist mostly of foreign diplomats and their families.

The modern attitude to religion has made for a significant change in funeral practices. Before the revolution a status-conscious Chinese would always buy an expensive coffin—sometimes years before his demise. And it was not unusual for the deceased to be tightly sealed into his coffin and left to lie in a temple for many months until a suitably auspicious burial site became available. Raucous professional mourners and chanting Taoist or Buddhist priests accompanied the hearse to the cemetery, where paper currency was burned to appease the spirits. Paper clothes, paper furniture and other simulated items were also burned for use in the afterlife. Nowadays, however, the deceased is likely to be laid out on a bicycle cart, covered with a quilt and trundled off to a crematorium.

Burial is still commonplace in country areas; but in Peking and other cities, space is too limited to spare for graveyards. Even the famous are usually cremated; and their ashes are stored in urns at the Pa Pao Shan cemetery on the western edge of the capital. It is still possible to see mourners squatting outside the gates of the cemetery, burning traditional offerings. But year by year their numbers grow fewer. Just as the Chinese way of life has adapted itself to the laws and conventions of the new regime, so, too, has the Chinese way of death.

Rare Images of a Vanished World

Seen from the south wall of Peking's Inner City in 1871, a thoroughfare leads into a mass of hovels. Beggars squat along the marble bridge in the foreground.

"Had Marco Polo been able to confirm by photographs his account of the wonders of Cathay, his fair fame would have escaped the discredit cast upon it for centuries." These words came from the pen of a world-roving Scotsman named John Thomson—author of numerous travel books, fellow of the Royal Geographical Society and, in 1871, one of the first men to turn a camera on China's capital. Like Marco Polo 600 years before him, Thomson was mesmerized by Peking's splendours, but he was also appalled by its backwardness. Nowhere else, he wrote, had he seen "poverty so wretched, ignorance so intense . . . . Filth seems to be deposited like tribute before the very palace gates." Using a wet-plate camera a cubic yard in size, he created a unique record—sampled on these pages—of a world that the revolutions of the 20th Century would consign to oblivion.

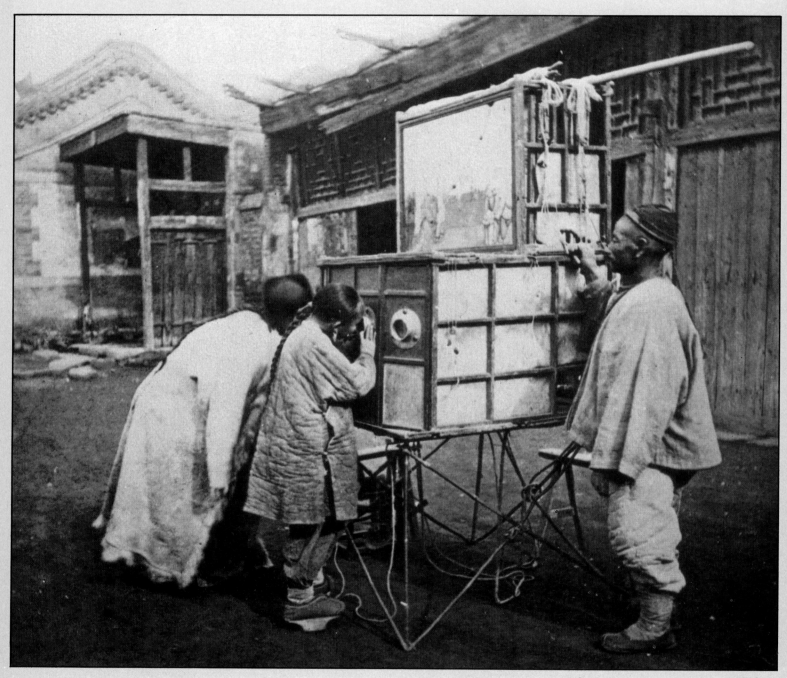

A favourite street entertainment in Peking was a risqué peep-show (above), whose operator delivered commentary while manipulating the interior scene by means of cords. Concluded Thomson: "The less one says the better."

Thomson admired the determination of poor Chinese, like this chiropodist at work by a roadside. "Many of them trade on nothing, living on nothing too, until by patience and thrift, they manage to obtain a fair living."

Beggars who have been hired by an undertaker
to inflate the size of the procession for a
soldier's funeral wait for the ceremonies to get
under way. The banners that they will carry
denote various corps of the Imperial army.

Beating a wooden clapper, a watchman in a
tattered coat answers a colleague's call.
Although the guard was allotted a decent salary
by the government, corrupt officials siphoned off
much of the money before it could reach him.

An upper-class Peking lady could spend hours having her hair dressed and white paste and pink powder put on her face. Then, said Thomson, she spent most of the remainder of her day gambling, gossiping and smoking opium.

A rich government official sits in the inner courtyard of his Peking home, surrounded by members of his family. Thomson described him as "a fine sample of the modern Chinese savant—fat, good-natured and contented".

3

Centuries of Splendour and Decadence

Peking has advanced at such an extraordinary pace since 1949 that a foreigner returning to this city for the first time since the Communist revolution might imagine that he had been transported forward in a time-machine. Within a single generation, the medieval-style city has become a 20th-Century metropolis. The lifestyle of its inhabitants has changed beyond all recognition and its physical fabric continues to undergo such rapid modernization that, by the end of this century, the old Peking will have disappeared almost completely.

Structurally, only one historic area in central Peking remains undisturbed: the 250 acres of the Forbidden City, which looks more or less as it did in the 15th Century when the Emperor Yung-lo conscripted a vast army of craftsmen and labourers to create for him an innermost sanctum-complex of palaces, temples, pavilions, ceremonial halls and libraries. But even this mini-city has changed in one essential; it is now more inviting than forbidding—an elaborate museum-piece that presents the largest and finest assemblage of Ming architecture in China.

Nowadays, for a small payment, anyone can enter via the great Wu Men, grandest of imperial gates where ordinary mortals were once compelled to kneel until the emperor, the Son of Heaven, gave permission for them to be admitted. They may even wander around the most holy of holies, the Hall of Supreme Harmony, where all officials and envoys, irrespective of status or nationality, could approach the Dragon Throne only by kowtowing—touching the floor nine times with their heads as a token of absolute submission to the emperor.

For more than 500 years the Hall of Supreme Harmony was regarded by a quarter of all mankind as the centre of the universe. Here, according to classic Chinese texts, "earth and sky meet, the four seasons merge, wind and rain are gathered in, and *yin* and *yang* are in harmony". Here, the Son of Heaven took his seat on ceremonial occasions to the accompaniment of gongs and jade chimes while, all around him, thick smoke of incense rose from cloisonné urns and from bronze figures of cranes and tortoises symbolizing long life. It was the throne room of a man-made god whose word was absolute: a despot who might order a man to be executed for the most trifling misdemeanour or who might sentence a more serious offender to be cut—literally—into ten thousand pieces.

That world of ostentatious barbarism now seems almost primeval. What meaning or relevance does it have today? Pondering Peking's imperial past while on a sightseeing tour of the Forbidden City (now designated

Sightseers descend a steep section of the Great Wall, a 4,000-mile long buttress built mainly in the 3rd Century B.C. to protect China from northern nomads. This portion, at the mountain pass of Pa-ta-ling about 25 miles north-west of Peking, has been restored by the government.

as the Palace Museum) is somewhat like strolling through Hampton Court Palace and trying to visualize some 16th-Century butchery commanded by Henry VIII. However, in this pleasure-palace, one is not looking back on some medieval madness but on a feudal way of life that dragged on into the 20th Century. Was it really only 1923 when the Forbidden City still had a population of some 1,500 eunuchs—attendants who managed to gain such influence and power at court that it was not unusual for ambitious or needy parents to have their male children castrated and then sold into the imperial household? Could it really be that as late as 1967 the last emperor of China died in the role of an obscure clerk devoting his days to serving the People's Republic? In modern Peking, city of rampant change, the imperial past has been rejected with a vengeance—yet it is very much a part of living memory.

To be able to appreciate the real character of the people of Peking—so resilient, adaptable and proud—it is important to get the city's past into proper perspective. As recently as 1949, this capital every night closed its gates on the outside world in the manner of some medieval fortress-city; and until that time, its people had never known a single year when they were not suffering under absolutist rule within or threatened by some belligerent force without. "Let the past serve the present," is one of the most oft-quoted thoughts from Chairman Mao's little red book; and Peking's past certainly serves the present as the supreme deterrent to any major deviation from the new political system.

The propaganda value of Peking's history is naturally exploited in the colossal Historical Museum on the east side of T'ien An Men Square. Here, ancient documents, drawings, maps and military hardware are arranged to emphasize how the city has been conquered and plundered by invaders from north, east, south and west; how it has been totally destroyed on four occasions; and how it has been governed (or more usually, misgoverned) by foreigners for fully half of the past millennium. The museum also holds wide-ranging art exhibits that illustrate the skill and industry of the simple craftsmen and, more pointedly, the self-indulgence of the old ruling classes who demanded unnecessary luxuries while millions of their people were overtaxed and underfed. The political message is inescapable—and for the most part, wholly justified.

Curiously, however, the most vivid impressions of Peking's turbulent past are not to be found within the city itself but in the surrounding countryside, especially towards the north-west—the direction of both the Valley of the Thirteen Ming Tombs and a section of the Great Wall of China. Here, far more than in the overwhelmingly didactic Historical Museum or even in the Forbidden City, the enormous excesses of pre-revolution Peking—the centuries of violence, suffering and privation, and extravagance—come within the compass of the mind's eye.

In this 18th-Century map, Peking is neatly bisected by massive walls (coloured grey) into two zones. The entire upper zone constitutes the Inner City, built between 1404 and 1421 as the capital of the Ming dynasty. Within it, the pink shaded area represents the walled grounds of the Imperial City; it, in turn, encloses the Forbidden City—indicated as a blank square surrounded by thick ramparts. The zone below the dividing wall is the Outer City, whose walls were constructed in the 16th Century to contain the southward sprawl of suburbs.

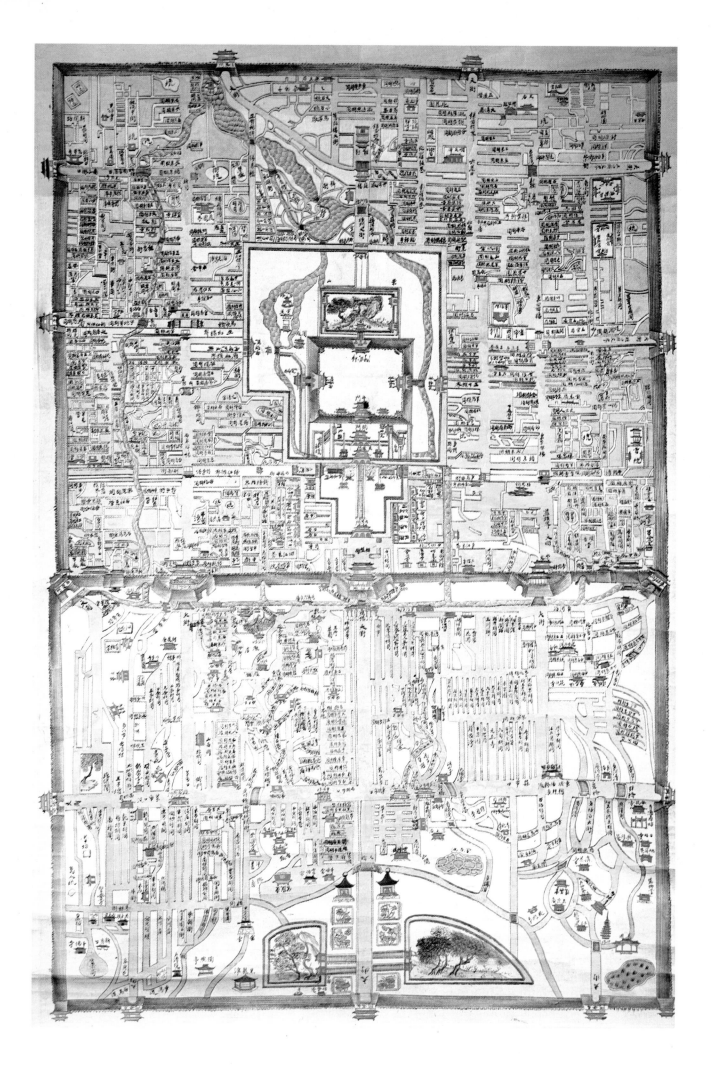

A visit to the Great Wall, 25 miles outside Peking, is the most logical introduction to the city's history. During the Chou dynasty (1122 to 256 B.C.), when the Wall was initiated as a series of watch-towers to guard the north frontier, Peking developed into an important garrison town named Chi. Its strategic importance became all the greater when Shih Huang-ti, First Sovereign Emperor of the Ch'in dynasty (221 to 209 B.C.), commanded the linking up of all the watch-towers and so secured his new, unified nation-state of China against barbarian tribes to the north.

The result of that command was the most massive man-made construction on earth: a battlemented serpent of stone, punctuated by some 25,000 towers, that twisted and turned for nearly 4,000 miles on its seemingly impossible obstacle course from the eastern coast at Shan-hai-kuan to Chiu-ch'üan near the Gobi Desert in the west. There is a feeling of great drama on seeing where this now-fragmented wall meets the sea, but its full magnificence is still to be viewed to best advantage near Peking—at Pa-ta-ling, beyond the Nan-k'ou Pass, where the astonishing structure, 30 feet high and 25 feet thick at the base, dips into great valleys and rises up steep mountainsides.

In summer, the dignity and mystique of this spot are degraded by hordes of day-trippers munching buns, guzzling fruit juice and basking in the sun. It is during winter, in below-freezing temperatures, that one really appreciates this greatest surviving symbol of oppression and human achievement. Then, standing on the battlements, lashed by ice-cold winds and hail, one can readily accept the unverified claim that half the hundreds of thousands of conscripted labourers died during its construction, and that the corpses of the workers were sometimes built into the Wall to placate the local spirits.

The Great Wall is an awesome sight—a fortification that should surely have made Peking impregnable in days of primitive warfare. But it was only as strong as the armies that manned it; and those armies were strong only as long as China's internal government remained united and resolute. Unfortunately for the people of Peking (let us, for convenience, use the city's post-14th-Century name), resolution was often lacking. Dynasties rose and fell; the country fragmented into conflicting states, re-united, and divided again. The Wall stood firm; but some northern tribes were about to surmount it without force of arms, relying instead on political guile and the treachery of Chinese commanders.

By the early 12th Century, Peking had fallen to a semi-nomadic group called Jürched, a Manchurian people from the Amur Valley in the far north. They took the dynastic name of Chin (meaning "golden") and in Peking, which they named Chung-tu (Central Capital), they created a city of imperial splendour with palaces to rival those of the Sung dynasty still in power in the south. The very magnificence and wealth of this new Chin nation eventually led to the total destruction of their capital.

A gatherer of firewood rides his bicycle past a 500-year-old stone elephant, one of 24 statues of animals that guard the road to the tombs of the Ming emperors 20 miles north of Peking. Framed by the elephant's trunk are two representations of a mythical beast called the "ch'i-lin", a benevolent creature of good omen.

In 1210 the prize of Peking lured from the north the most feared military campaigner in Asia: Genghis Khan, the Mongol leader whose greatest joy was—in his own words—"to conquer one's enemies, to pursue them, to seize their property, to see their families in tears, to ride their horses, and to possess their daughters and wives". His nomadic and primitive people totally lacked the kind of culture and artistic refinement that flourished in China; and yet, in terms of military strength, skill and mobility, they were infinitely superior.

Even the Great Khan was at first over-awed by the Great Wall. For two years he waited menacingly in the region of Jehol, 120 miles to the north. Meanwhile, in an effort to buy time to flee south and make his capital at K'ai-feng on the Yellow River, the Chin emperor stalled the Mongol leader with gifts. Genghis Khan demanded more, and he received more: a thousand young men and girls, three thousand horses, vast quantities of gold and jewellery. Then, on learning that the imperial court had deserted the city, he ordered an all-out attack. His hordes broke through the Great Wall by sheer force of numbers and at terrible cost to both sides. In May, 1215, they stormed the walls of Peking itself, leaving the capital in ruins—every building razed to the ground, all its people massacred.

In the same year, Kublai Khan, grandson of Genghis Khan, was born. He was destined to rule an empire that extended from the Pacific to the Dnepr River in Russia, from the Arctic Ocean to the Strait of Malacca. In 1256 he commanded the building of a summer capital, Xanadu, in hill country on the fringe of the Gobi Desert. And in 1260, against all probability, he chose Peking as the site for his winter capital. Seven years later he ordered its reconstruction—as a city to be named Ta-tu (Great Capital). "In Xanadu," wrote the opium-drugged English poet Samuel

Coleridge, "did Kublai Khan a stately pleasure-dome decree." In Peking he decreed much more. By 1270, it had become a city of unrivalled opulence—a vast complex of palaces, courtyards, gardens, artificial lakes and hills—with a population of 400,000 registered citizens. The following year he proclaimed the beginning of a new Chinese dynasty entitled Ta Yüan (Great Origin), with himself as the first emperor.

The Peking of the Mongols rose behind a square of six-mile-long walls, with the main palace and arsenal situated behind an inner square of walls guarded by fortified towers. Twelve thousand horsemen made up the emperor's personal guard; and 3,000 were permanently on duty at the central palace. Here, Kublai Khan held feasts of Arabian Nights splendour in a banqueting hall that could seat 6,000 guests; and here, every New Year's Day, his 5,000 elephants were paraded in stately procession, together with a huge herd of camels.

Basically, the Mongols changed nothing in China, while they themselves were changed in many ways. Like the alien rulers who came after them, they found it expedient to retain the Chinese way of administering the country through an élite class of bureaucrats. The Chinese were allowed to continue their own traditions in architecture, art and music. Meanwhile, to appear less foreign, the Mongols adopted Chinese dress and manners, and they even prayed in Chinese temples for fine harvests. As for other foreigners, Kublai Khan carefully segregated them from the natives of the city. Even though the Mongol emperor was anxious to learn foreign technology and to trade with other nations, it was accepted that the foreign caravans arriving in Peking should be restricted to isolated areas in the outskirts of the city and should be treated with the utmost caution, suspicion, and disdain.

The Yüan dynasty lasted just 108 years. Kublai Khan's descendants made civil war inevitable when they imposed crippling taxes on a people already reduced to near-starvation by a series of appalling floods and other natural disasters. Many rebel groups rose up to defy the Mongol oppressors, the most powerful of them led by Chu Yüan-chang, a one-time Buddhist monk who had been born a peasant. In 1368 he marched north with an army to capture the Mongols' winter capital and proclaim the beginning of the Ming (meaning "brilliant") dynasty. The ex-peasant Chu took for himself the name of Hung Wu (Vast Military Power), renamed the conquered city Pei-p'ing (Northern Peace), and chose as his capital Nanking, 580 miles to the south.

China had a native emperor once more. Yet this held no great significance for the common people. The centuries-old system of absolutist government was so firmly entrenched that peasant uprisings never brought the slightest movement towards constitutional government. The triumphant rebels merely formed a new hierarchy that became no less tyrannical than that of their predecessors. In some ways their reign was even more puritanical—and it was far more enduring: Ming emperors ruled, with varying degrees of brilliance or incompetence, for almost three centuries, from 1368 to 1644.

The best way to sense the scope and splendour of this dynasty is to visit the Valley of the Thirteen Ming Tombs—an extraordinarily enchanting resting place 20 miles north-west of the city. The charm of this valley lies partly in its final approach along the Great Spirit Way—an avenue lined with massive sculptures of warriors, elephants, camels, horses and mythological beasts—but most particularly in the utter tranquillity and picturesque beauty of the unexcavated tomb sites. The pavilions in front of the great oval burial mounds are ochre-red, with remnants of coloured tiled roofs dominated by imperial yellow. The sky, on most days, is an intense, unclouded blue. Tiny wild flowers add specks of pink and mauve to the scene, and bluish pine trees stand around in attitudes suggesting antiquity. Yet, overall, the setting has a distinctly timeless quality, as if one had stepped into some magical realm.

The greatest disturbance one is likely to encounter here is the arrival of a party of foreign diplomats and journalists with picnic hampers and corkscrews. Even then, there are enough deserted tomb sites—each a mile or so apart—to escape completely from the day-tripping crowds. But one is never quite alone in this exquisite area; usually a pair of Chinese public security officials, blue-coated and wearing dark glasses, will trail you on a motor-cycle at a discreet distance. The surveillance prevents visitors from taking souvenirs from the many loose ceramic tiles that have fallen to the ground.

For many visitors, the supreme experience in Peking used to be a night picnic at the Ming Tombs. They would come bearing little oil lamps and lounge among the slabs of fabulous old masonry, reading poetry or singing songs as the darkness closed in. But this delightful pastime was forbidden by the Peking authorities in 1975, perhaps because the security men objected to having to sit, shivering, on their motor-bikes while foreigners capered around—or perhaps because erotic passion too obviously over-took some of the carousers. In any event, these nocturnal high jinks were hardly fitting in an imperial burial ground.

All but three of the 16 Ming emperors were entombed in this valley, together with their empresses and favourite concubines. The largest of all the tombs belongs to Yung-lo, fourth son of the peasant-turned-emperor Chu Yüan-chang. It was Yung-lo who moved the seat of imperial government from Nanking back to Pei'ping and gave the capital—for the first time—the name of Peking. At his command, the city was almost completely reconstructed, with greater magnificence than ever before. And it is this city, completed in 1421, that we can see today within the walls of the Inner City and the Forbidden City, and—two miles to the south —at the Temple of Heaven (the supreme example of Ming architecture),

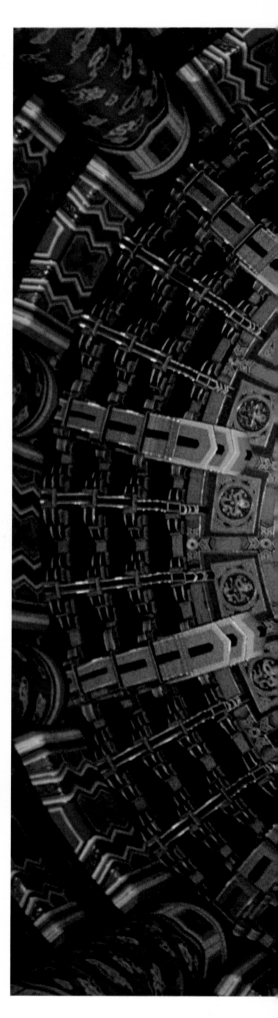

In imperial times China's rulers went each
spring to the Hall of Prayer for Good Harvests
(above), in the Temple of Heaven complex
located in south-east Peking, and there
interceded with the gods for bountiful crops.
Today tourists visit the building—reconstructed
after fire destroyed the original 15th-century
hall in 1889—to admire its harmonious
architecture and elaborate domed roof (right).

which emperors visited each winter to worship and each spring to offer sacrifices and prayers for rich harvests.

Yung-lo usually did things on the grand scale. He commissioned the largest encyclopaedia ever compiled—the Yung-lo ta-tien, comprising more than 11,000 manuscript volumes. (The project kept around 2,000 scholars employed full-time for four years—and then only three copies of the work were ever made.) He was the emperor who sent the eunuch Admiral Cheng Ho on seven great voyages of discovery. Some 60 years before Columbus began his voyage to the New World with three modest-sized vessels and about a hundred men, Cheng was commanding a fleet with some 20,000 men that sailed to India, to the South Seas, and as far as the East African coast. But Yung-lo, in spite of bearing a name that meant "Perpetual Happiness", was a despot of the first order. The rebuilding of Peking, the commissioning of works of arts, the despatching of his fleet to bring back such curiosities as zebras, ostriches and giraffes—all such acts were for self-gratification or self-glorification.

Beginning with Yung-lo, eunuchs—employed as imperial servants since the days of the Han dynasty (206 B.C. to A.D. 220)—became ever more numerous and powerful. Within the Forbidden City, princes grew up with eunuchs as their exclusive friends through childhood and often became dependent on these substitute "father-figures" when they succeeded to the Dragon Throne. This was especially true of Emperor Wan-li, a pampered child when he came to the throne in 1572. His reign lasted nearly 50 years, the longest of any of the Ming emperors. It was a period renowned for its cultural brilliance. But the ruler himself contributed nothing to this brilliance; always self-indulgent, he absorbed himself in a world of private extravagance, totally cut off from his subjects, isolated in a court that included, according to Chinese records, 9,000 palace women and as many as 70,000 eunuchs.

At the age of 22, Wan-li ordered the building of a palatial tomb that would surround him in death with as much grandeur as he knew in life. It took four years to construct and he celebrated its completion by holding a lavish banquet within it. This is now the one excavated mausoleum in the Valley of the Ming Tombs, having been opened up in 1956 to reveal five great halls covering about 1,200 square metres. In one of the halls were found three red-lacquered coffins (holding the remains of the emperor and two empresses) surrounded by 26 chests of jewels and personal possessions. Nowadays a notice posted near the plain stone staircase leading down to the tomb reminds visitors that this underground palace was built at a cost of eight million ounces of silver and enough manpower to have produced grain to feed a million people for six years.

After Wan-li's death, an inept 15-year-old ascended the throne and eunuchs virtually ruled all of China until 1627, when the last great Ming emperor, Ch'ung Chen, came to power. But the Ming dynasty—after so

The Phoenix Capital

8th Century B.C.	Chou-dynasty city of Chi grows on site of modern Peking as a garrison for soldiers defending the northern frontier against marauding nomadic tribes
551	Chinese philosopher Confucius born
221	China unified under Ch'in dynasty; Chi assumes status of provincial trading centre
214	Completion of 4,000-mile-long Great Wall by the tyrant-emperor, Shih Huang-ti
A.D. 605	Grand Canal, 1,000 miles long, links Chi with Yangtze Valley
618	With the founding of the T'ang dynasty, Chi renamed Yu-chou and develops in importance as a frontier city
936	Khitan Mongols from Manchuria, founders of Liao dynasty, destroy Yu-chou and build a new city on the same site. Called Nan-ching (Southern Capital), it also receives the literary name of Yen-ching (Swallow Capital)
1153	Jürched nomads from Manchuria conquer Yen-ching and rename it Chung-tu (Central Capital). During their brief rule—period of the Chin dynasty—the walls are expanded and the city is adorned with splendid palaces.
1215	Genghis Khan, founder of a vast Mongol empire, sweeps down from the north to capture and raze Chung-tu
1260	Kublai Khan, grandson of Genghis, elected ruler of Mongols and proclaims start of Yüan dynasty
1264	Construction of new city of Ta-tu (Great Capital) begins just north-east of ruined Chung-tu; city walls are completed three years later
1270	Population of Ta-tu reaches 400,000
1275	Venetian traveller Marco Polo visits court of Kublai Khan in Ta-tu
1368	Peasant army under the Chinese leader Chu Yüan-chang captures Ta-tu and overthrows Mongols. Under the new Ming (Brilliant) dynasty, Ta-tu is renamed Pei-p'ing (Northern Peace) and gives up its status as a capital to Nanking in the south
1403	Despotic Emperor Yung-lo, son of rebel leader Chu, decides to move capital back to Pei-p'ing, now renamed Peking (Northern Capital)
1404	Yung-lo launches massive reconstruction of Peking. Within two decades, the walled Imperial and Forbidden Cities are built largely on the lines seen today
1550-65	Southern suburbs of Peking walled in to create the Outer City
1601	Italian Jesuit Matteo Ricci permitted to set up first Catholic mission in Peking
1644	Manchu rebel Li Tzu-ch'eng captures Peking, and last Ming emperor, Chuang-lieh-ti, commits suicide on Coal Hill. Ch'ing (Pure) dynasty established
1651	White Dagoba, a Buddhist temple, constructed on Emerald Isle in Pei Hai Park
1793	British diplomat Lord Macartney visits Peking in unsuccessful attempt to establish embassy in city and forge stronger trade links with China
1839	Opium War breaks out between China and Britain; concluded by Treaty of Nanking three years later
1856	Second Anglo-Chinese conflict erupts and is ended by Treaty of Tientsin two years later. Pact grants Western nations right to set up legations in Peking
1860	After European envoys are refused permission to enter Peking, Britain and France send troops to enforce terms of Tientsin treaty. Peking is occupied

many years of misgovernment—was already doomed. The country was in general disorder, threatened by rebellion and invasion. In the north, from the region we know today as Manchuria, a new group of nomads, the Manchu, were pressing down to seize advantage of China's internal chaos. Unlike the Mongols, the Manchu did not immediately triumph. Peking stood firm against their assaults in 1629 and again in 1638. But in 1644, Chinese rebels succeeded in taking the city with the aid of a treacherous eunuch official. The last Ming emperor hanged himself from a locust tree on Coal Hill, overlooking his beloved Forbidden City.

In desperation, a Ming army commander enlisted the aid of the Manchu to recover the capital from the rebels. The effect of this partnership with foreigners was to seal the end of the last native Chinese imperial line. After the Manchu took Peking, they kept it strictly for themselves, making it their capital and expanding their control and authority throughout the empire. For their dynasty they took the name Ch'ing (meaning "pure"). They were to rule for the next 267 years.

With rare exceptions, China had denied entry to all foreigners ("barbarians") during the Ming regime. This curtain of isolation from the rest of the world continued to be held down in the Ch'ing dynasty. In the late 18th Century foreigners were still not allowed to live in China, and they could conduct trade only from certain specified ports in the far south—notably Canton and Macao. The export of all Chinese books was prohibited, and it was a criminal offence for a Chinese to teach his language to a foreigner. Moreover, the Chinese eschewed Western knowledge: the ruling class, as always, was educated in the classics of Chinese literature and discouraged from the study of such subjects as economics and science. Through this policy of inwardness, the country that had once led the world in inventiveness (the crossbow, cast iron, the stern rudder, gunpowder, the magnetic compass, paper and movable type were all Chinese creations) became the retarded child among great nations.

China's attitude to foreigners can be most clearly illustrated by the treatment of the British diplomat Lord Macartney, who was sent to Peking in 1793 to petition for stronger trade links and the establishment of diplomatic relations. He sailed with a great retinue and all manner of gifts for the elderly Manchu emperor, Ch'ien-lung: a planetarium, a hot-air balloon, scientific instruments, an assortment of clocks and watches. On arrival he was politely informed that he would be expected to kowtow to the emperor in traditional style. This involved kneeling three times and, after each kneeling, casting oneself forward three times so that the forehead touched the ground. The ritual seemed more like grovelling than paying respect; and Lord Macartney declined to do so, unless a Chinese official of equal rank did likewise to a portrait of his king, George III. Finally, a compromise was reached: it was agreed that the

A few crumbling ruins in north-west Peking are all that remain of the "European Palaces"— sumptuous summer residences built in the 1740s for Emperor Ch'ien-lung from designs by an Italian Jesuit attached to his court. The palaces, the largest of which is shown in the 18th-century engraving reproduced above, were razed by British troops in 1860, as retaliation for the mistreatment of prisoners by the Chinese.

British ambassador should do obeisance by a simple genuflection—with the reservation that he should not kiss the emperor's hand, as would be the custom in the "Western Ocean" courts.

Macartney and his aides were royally entertained by the 82-year-old emperor. "I have seen 'King Solomon' in all his glory," the diplomat wrote in his diary after attending a five-hour banquet with non-stop distractions—wrestling, acrobatics, wire-dancing, play-acting and fireworks. Yet his mission accomplished absolutely nothing. George III's requests were never properly discussed. After weeks of inactivity, Macartney at last received a response. A procession of officials and servants arrived at his quarters ceremoniously bearing a yellow silk armchair; on the chair lay the emperor's written reply to George III: "We have never valued ingenious articles, nor do we have the slightest need of your country's manufactures. . . . You, O King, should simply act in conformity with our wishes by strengthening your loyalty and swearing perpetual obedience so as to ensure that your country may share the blessings of peace."

There is no reason to suppose that Macartney failed through his refusal to kowtow. Previous embassies from Europe correctly humbled themselves and still left without benefits for their countries. Shortly after the British diplomat had departed, two Dutch envoys arrived in Peking. They prostrated themselves on no fewer than 30 occasions. One of them, André Everard van Braam, amused the emperor no end; he kowtowed on a frozen roadside as the Son of Heaven was carried past, humbling himself so energetically that his wig fell off. The result, however, was exactly the same: a total lack of interest in developing overseas trade.

Old Ch'ien-lung had overlooked just one item when he told George III that China needed none of the manufactures of Great Britain or her colonies. It was the British—seeking to counterbalance their huge imports of silk fabrics and China tea—who exploited the one commodity irresistible to many Chinese. In the early 17th Century the Chinese had begun to mix opium with tobacco and smoke it—a practice ineffectively banned by imperial edict in 1729. Now the demand for opium had risen to a significant level and it was greatly encouraged by Britain, whose East India Company had the world's richest poppy-growing estates in Bengal. Mainly through British and American merchants operating in Canton, opium was smuggled into China in ever increasing quantities—420,000 pounds in 1816, almost 700,000 pounds in 1820, nearly 1,400,000 pounds in 1825. Ten years later, the imports had risen to 5,600,000 pounds and China had an estimated two million addicts, the majority drawn from the upper classes and many of them officials who could easily be corrupted by the drug runners.

Now, for the first time in China's history, the value of her imports exceeded that of her exports, and precious silver was flowing out of the country at a rate that threatened economic catastrophe. Peking appointed

Beneath an inscription wishing her long life, the Empress Dowager Tz'u-hsi, who ruled China through a series of regencies from 1861 until her death in 1908, poses with the wives of European diplomats. This photograph, taken towards the end of her life, was the first in which the xenophobic Empress Dowager consented to appear with foreigners.

an Imperial Commissioner for the Suppression of the Opium Trade and, in 1839, he seized and destroyed some 2,800,000 pounds of opium belonging to British merchants in Canton. Soon afterwards Britain used a minor judicial dispute as an excuse for launching a punitive action—the so-called Opium War—that eventually was ended in 1842 by the ludicrously unjust Treaty of Nanking. China was compelled by the peace terms to cede to Great Britain the island of Hong Kong, to open up five ports for unrestricted foreign trade and residence, and to pay an indemnity of 21 million silver dollars for a war she had never sought. The treaty mentioned opium not at all.

In 1858, a second Anglo-Chinese conflict ended in the Treaty of Tientsin that opened up more ports for British trade, stipulated an indemnity of four million silver dollars and—most alarming to the Manchu court—gave Britain the right to conduct diplomatic relations "on terms of equality" and to have a British minister resident in Peking. Two years later, in order to force the ratification of this treaty (under its terms trading privileges had also been conceded to France, Russia and the United States), the British and French governments ordered their expeditionary forces to march on Peking. Yet again, the ancient capital was to be pillaged and destroyed by foreign invaders.

A few miles north-west of Peking, the French troops came upon the Yüan Ming Yüan (Garden of Perfection and Light)—an astonishing assemblage of scarlet and gold halls, pavilions, artificial hills and lakes, and a wondrous system of ornate fountains. Here was the incomparable Summer Palace completed in the reign of Emperor Ch'ien-lung—a pleasure garden that has been described as the "Chinese Versailles". In fact, it was designed with the help of Jesuits in the Italian style of the late 17th Century, and it ranked as one of the most ingenious blends of Chinese and Western culture ever achieved.

On arrival at the Yüan Ming Yüan, the French soldiers went into a frenzy of looting, officers and men alike scrambling for myriad Chinese treasures—precious jewels, gold and silver, enamel screens and porcelain vases, silver clocks, music-boxes, mechanical toys. Lord Elgin, the British envoy, later wrote: "Plundering and devastating a place like this is bad enough, but what is much worse is the wastage and breakage. . . . French soldiers were destroying in every way the most beautiful silks, breaking the jade ornaments and porcelain. War is a hateful business. . . ."

But then Elgin learned the gory details of atrocities performed by the Chinese on French and British prisoners. Pondering what form the reprisals should take, he finally decided that the total destruction of the Yüan Ming Yüan—the emperor's favourite residence—would have the most telling impact. So British troops, on his command, razed the magnificent Summer Palace—more than 200 pavilions, halls and temples and fountains. (Ironically, Elgin's father, 40 years earlier, had saved from destruction by the Turks the classic Greek sculptures of the Parthenon in Athens—the so-called Elgin Marbles.)

For a Westerner, the Yüan Ming Yüan is still one of the most fascinating spots in the Peking area. Its ruins stand near a goat-herding commune, not far from the city's Ch'ing-hua University of Science and Technology, and its attraction lies partly in the sheer incongruity of its setting. Jolting over a log bridge (presuming you can find the obscure turn-off), you drive past the remnants of the old water reservoir and suddenly you find yourself amid a scene that, by all rights, belongs somewhere on the outskirts of Rome. Neo-classical pillars and arches, seemingly on the point of collapse, rise out of a jumble of fallen, shrub-covered marble. Grass hollows provide perfect snuggeries for picnicking in the shadow of what was once a lovely fountain.

Not far from the pathetic ruins of the Yüan Ming Yüan, another Summer Palace can be seen. Located seven miles north-west of the Forbidden City, it is a lasting monument to the extravagances and follies of the most remarkable woman in the history of imperial China. Her name was Tz'u-hsi, meaning "Motherly and Auspicious". In 1852, as the 16-year-old daughter of a minor mandarin, she became a fifth-rank concubine, one of 28 Manchu girls selected for the harem of the Emperor Hsien-feng.

Four years later she won the race to provide the dropsical young sovereign with his first son. Then, five years further on, when the emperor died, she became the Empress Dowager and assumed absolute power over an empire of 400 million people. Incredibly, by engineering a series of regencies, she held on to that power for almost half a century.

It is difficult to separate fact from fiction when it comes to this last omnipotent ruler of the Chinese Empire. Stories of her debauchery are legion and mostly impossible to substantiate. But certainly there were no limits to her ruthlessness and avarice. She was sadistic, supremely cunning and, above all, excessively vain. She once observed: "I have often thought that I am the cleverest woman who ever lived. . . . Although I have heard much about Queen Victoria . . . I don't think her life is half as interesting and eventful as mine." But Tz'u-hsi's life in Peking was dedicated entirely to pomp and ceremony and the pursuit of pleasure and power; and by her self-indulgence and double-dealing she did more than anyone to hasten the end of the dynastic system in China.

An imitation paddle-steamer made of marble adorns the lakefront at the old Imperial Summer Palace outside Peking. Three decades after the palace was burned and looted by the British in 1860, the Empress Dowager Tz'u-hsi remodelled it by drawing on funds intended for China's antiquated navy. This elegant folly was the only "boat" built with the money.

In 1888, the Empress Dowager—or "the Old Buddha" as she was generally known—insisted on building a new Summer Palace to replace her beloved Yüan Ming Yüan. She had a passion for water picnics, and so she decreed that the vast pleasure complex should include a palace beside an artificial lake and a two-storey marble pavilion rising from the water in the shape of a Mississippi paddle-steamer. It was a time of grave economic crisis and so, very properly, she announced that the project would be financed out of her private savings and "entail no expense or sacrifice to the country". She then appropriated the necessary sum—roughly $50 million—from the funds that had been budgeted for building a modern Chinese navy. Tz'u-hsi got her marble paddle-steamer, and it still stands secure today. However, China's antiquated navy was destroyed by a modernized Japanese fleet in 1895.

That naval defeat compelled "the Old Buddha" to make a rare sacrifice: she cancelled the elaborate Peking celebrations of her 60th birthday. Bitterly, she railed: "Who would have anticipated that the dwarf men [the Japanese] would have dared to force us into hostilities?" Certainly, it would have been unthinkable just two decades before. But the reign of the Empress Dowager had reduced China to a sick giant, desperately in need of internal reforms. The humiliation in the Sino-Japanese War greatly worsened the country's plight. The price of peace was the cession of the island of Formosa, the surrender of suzerainty over Korea, and an indemnity of 200 million silver dollars, as well as the opening of four more ports to foreign trade.

At this point in history, China was encircled by foreign powers as never before. The French controlled all of Vietnam. The British occupied Burma and Hong Kong. The Russians had expanded their Siberian and Central Asian territories, and had established a dominant position in the Manchurian province. More ominously, in 1896, the Russians moved into Port Arthur, 280 miles east of Peking; and the Germans used the murder of two of their Roman Catholic missionaries as an excuse for grabbing the port of Kiaochow on the Yellow Sea.

By all logic, it was a time for skilled international diplomacy to allow China opportunity to regain strength. Instead, the Empress Dowager became more xenophobic than ever. In 1898, her young nephew, the sickly and high-strung Emperor Kuang-hsü, listened to reformists and briefly tried to exercise his own authority. She promptly ordered him confined under "palace arrest" for the rest of his life. The following year she proclaimed: "The various powers cast upon us looks of tiger-like voracity, hustling each other in their endeavours to be the first to seize upon our innermost territories. They think that China, having neither money nor troops, would never venture to go to war with them. . . . Never should the word 'Peace' fall from the mouths of our highest officials. . . . With such a country as ours, with her vast area . . . her immense natural resources, and her hundreds of millions of inhabitants, if all would prove their loyalty to the emperor and love of their country, what indeed is there to fear from any strong invader? Let us not think of making peace, nor rely solely upon diplomatic manoeuvres."

Throughout 1899, following increased miseries due to drought and then flood, anti-foreign riots had been breaking out in the northern provinces with ever-growing frequency. Most violent of all were gangs of red-turbaned, red-coated youths—members of a group called I-ho T'uan, or the Society of the Righteous and Harmonious Fists—who sought to restore their country's power and dignity through a mass movement that was directed against foreign influences. These fanatics actually convinced each other that, through magical rituals, they could make themselves bullet-proof; and because these rituals included shadow-boxing exercises, they became known as the Boxers.

In many ways, the Boxers may be seen as the precursors of the Red Guards of the 1960s—those young radicals who, with Mao Tse-tung's encouragement, attempted to stamp out all vestiges of "bourgeois" life during the so-called Cultural Revolution. Both movements turned their greatest wrath against foreigners and those who "fawned" on foreigners. In 1900, the target group included thousands of Chinese Christians who accepted foreign protection in return for their religious conversion.

Tz'u-hsi's reactions to the crisis were impossibly ambivalent. She ordered the recruitment of voluntary militia to help defend China against foreign "aggression". At the same time, fearing the consequences of international conflict, she emphasized that foreigners—diplomats, merchants and missionaries—should be accorded the rights and protection granted to them under various treaties. She could not immediately approve of the Boxers' rampaging acts of violence, but she was loath to discourage them. After all, the Boxers were unlike the many secret societies that had launched uprisings in China before. These peasants were not rebelling against the Establishment; on the contrary, they swore absolute loyalty to the ruling Ch'ing dynasty and so supported the corrupt government that was responsible for the desperate plight of the masses.

Gathering supporters and massacring Christian missionaries and converts as they moved further north, the Boxers reached the gates of Peking at the end of May, 1900. On June 9, the grandstand of Peking racecourse —a symbol of foreign "privilege"—was burned down. On June 11, the chancellor at the Japanese Legation was murdered by Chinese soldiers and his mutilated body with the heart cut out was left in a street gutter. On June 13, the Boxers began to run riot through the streets, slaughtering hundreds of defenceless Chinese Christians, burning churches, and razing all shops that sold foreign goods.

Three days earlier an eight-nation relief force of some 2,000 sailors and marines under the British admiral Sir Edward Seymour had set out

Amid the grounds of the old Summer Palace, a seventeen-arch bridge rising over the misty waters of K'un-ming Lake links an artificial island to the shore.

for Peking from the port of Tientsin. But now they were driven back to the sea by both Boxers and Chinese troops. Meanwhile, a thousand foreigners and 3,000 Chinese servants and converts took refuge in the hastily fortified Legation Quarter, immediately south-east of the Imperial City, and waited for the relief column to save them. They were to remain there under siege for 55 terrifying days, during which they were defended only by four small artillery pieces and a garrison of some 400 soldiers of various nationalities. More remarkably, at an isolated cathedral in north Peking, an equal number of people—priests, nuns, converts and children—were to hold out under siege with the support of only 40 troops.

On June 19 the Chinese authorities issued an ultimatum. Within the next 24 hours, the foreign residents could have safe conduct to Tientsin; thereafter they stayed on at their peril. G. E. Morrison, correspondent in Peking for *The Times* of London and a heroic figure in the siege, strongly opposed accepting the offer. It would mean abandoning to certain death the thousands of faithful Chinese under foreign protection. But only one leading diplomat (the German minister, Baron von Ketteler) supported him, and so it was decided to accept. The Corps Diplomatique replied that they were willing to leave, but they needed more than one day to prepare for the departure and they wanted an immediate interview to discuss the arrangements.

Next morning Baron von Ketteler grew impatient for the Chinese reply. He said he would hurry them up by calling in person at the Chinese Bureau of Foreign Affairs about a mile away. Accompanied by an interpreter, he set off in his official sedan chair down the silent, fire-scarred streets. On the way, a Manchu soldier rode up and shot the minister in the head at point blank range. The German interpreter, himself wounded in both legs, dragged himself back to the Legation Quarter to tell the story; and from that moment there was no further talk about accepting the offer of safe conduct. The siege of Peking was on in earnest.

On June 21, the Empress Dowager decreed, in the emperor's name, that China was at war with Britain, the United States, France, Germany, Italy, Austria, Belgium, Holland and Japan. According to her, the war had been precipitated by the European forces under Admiral Seymour; these forces, she said, were demanding the surrender of forts that guarded the approach to the port of Tientsin. In fact, the forts had already fallen into Allied hands after a brief and bloodless battle.

Tz'u-hsi further explained: "Ever since the foundation of the dynasty, foreigners coming to China have been kindly treated. In the reigns of Tso-kuang and Hsien-feng they were allowed to trade, and to propagate their religion. At first they were amenable to Chinese control, but for the past 30 years they have taken advantage of our forbearance to encroach on our territory, to trample on the Chinese people, and to absorb the wealth of the Empire. Every concession made only serves to increase their insolence. They oppress our peaceful subjects, and insult the gods and sages, exciting indignation among the people. . . . Hence the burning of chapels and the slaughter of converts. . . ."

Tz'u-hsi now described the Boxers as "patriotic soldiers", but she was less enthusiastic when they forced a way into the Forbidden City and struck the court's eunuchs and maids on the foreheads with their fists in the belief that, if they were secret Christians, the resulting bruises would appear in the shape of a cross. By July 1, she was calling the Boxers "untrained bandits". In mid-July, after ordering a ceasefire in the sieges of the Legation Quarter and the cathedral, she switched her position yet again. She was a victim of circumstances, she said; the Boxers were to blame. Artfully, she had cartloads of provisions and other supplies sent into the beleaguered Legation Quarter and ordered lists of foreign casualties and damaged property to be drawn up.

Then, on July 29, the siege was resumed. The Empress Dowager hoped for a complete massacre, leaving no witnesses who could challenge her version of the conflict. But it was too late. Once again united foreign powers were marching on Peking, now as a relief force comprising 8,000 Japanese troops, 4,500 Russians, 3,000 British, 2,500 Americans and 800 French. The vanguard of the column arrived on August 14. This time the foreign troops did not destroy a Summer Palace beyond the city walls: they invaded the Forbidden City itself and engaged in wild looting and arson, while the sacred Temple of Heaven was desecrated by being turned into a barracks.

As the foreign troops were fighting their way to Peking, the Empress Dowager escaped from the palace, riding in a simple wagon and dressed in the dark blue cottons of a peasant, with her lacquered nails cut back from their former six-inch length and her elaborate hair ornaments removed. Her nephew, the 28-year-old emperor, rode meekly behind in a second wagon. There was no room for the imperial concubines; and the old aunt had such hatred for her nephew's favourite, the Pearl Concubine that, just as she was about to leave the Forbidden City, she ordered her eunuchs to drown the young woman in a well in the north-east section of the palace. Then, after calling at the new Summer Palace to arrange for treasures to be taken north of the Great Wall, she continued on in her "imperial Chariot", enduring two months of rough riding until she had travelled 700 miles south-west to Sian.

Peking was now a disaster area divided into sections separately administered by individual foreign powers. Few Chinese remained in the capital. Countless hundreds had committed suicide rather than face the vengeful foreigners; the majority had taken to the hills. The plundering and destruction continued for weeks, and worse came in late September with the arrival of a German force bent on avenging the assassination of Baron von Ketteler. The Kaiser had exhorted his troops to comport themselves so that "just as the Huns one thousand years ago, under the leadership of Attila, gained a reputation by virtue of which they still live in historical tradition, so may the name of Germany become known in such a manner in China". Attila would have been proud of them; they publicly decapitated the Baron's assassin and then set out from Peking on punitive and plundering expeditions.

In 1901 a peace treaty created a fortified legation district in Peking, gave the foreign powers still more control and influence in China, and imposed a war indemnity of $739 million, to be paid in instalments by 1940. Only the United States, of the eight powers concerned, had the foresight to argue that this indemnity should be reduced by more than one-third. As it was, this sum—on top of the Sino-Japanese War indemnity of 1895—served only to ensure that China would be financially crippled for decades and still less able to bring about the social and economic reforms so necessary to relieve the poverty of the masses and to create a more stable society.

But the Empress Dowager suffered not at all. The Boxers and corrupt princes and ministers of state were, she said, entirely responsible for that midsummer madness in Peking. In 1902 she returned in grand style to her capital and began to make long overdue reforms. Footbinding became illegal. She abolished confessions by torture and capital punishment by ten thousand cuts. She established a Ministry of Commerce and revised the system of civil service examinations that had survived since A.D. 622. She decreed that there would be study of history, sciences and geography as well as the Confucian classics; and scholars would be selected to attend advanced studies in Japanese and Western universities. She also introduced a 10-year plan for the suppression of opium traffic. Most important of all, she dispatched a commission of inquiry to Europe, the United States and Japan to study constitutional government. Subsequently, it was planned that China should have a constitutional monarch from 1917 onwards.

However, it was all too late to save the Manchu dynasty. The spirit of the republican movement—led by Sun Yat-sen, a doctor-turned-revolutionary—was spreading far and wide. It gained fresh momentum on November 14, 1908, when the ineffectual, aunt-dominated emperor died. That day Tz'u-hsi chose his successor: a two-year-old child, P'u-yi, the son of the emperor's brother. For the third time she was arranging to have a boy under the age of six propped up on pillows on the Dragon Throne. Early that month "the Old Buddha" had celebrated her seventy-third birthday, announcing that she had every intention of surpassing the years of the late Queen Victoria. But on November 15, the first day of the new regency, she had a seizure and died.

The mood throughout the whole country was now intensely radical. A thousand rebellions had failed to change the basic structure of Chinese

In a fan-shaped German political cartoon, troops of eight nations join to put down the Boxer Rebellion, an uprising against foreign influences that swept through China in 1900. The allied soldiers—whose ranks, as seen in the photograph at right, included colonial recruits—had more difficulty in suppressing the revolt than the cartoon would suggest: European residents of Peking had to endure a 55-day siege before a relief force rescued them.

rule, but total revolution had finally become inevitable. It erupted in the south on October 10, 1911. Province after province, in swift succession, declared independence from the Manchu court. On December 28, the imperial family was again forced to flee the capital; and two months later it was announced that the boy-emperor was abdicating in favour of the new constitutional republic. More than 2,000 years of imperial rule in China had at last come to an end.

The Republic of Dr. Sun Yat-sen, with Nanking as the new capital, was virtually doomed from the start. China, in 1912, was still hopelessly divided into separate regions by rival generals, warlords or politicians, and within a year Dr. Sun had bowed out to the one man who might conceivably be strong enough to prevent civil war: Yüan Shih-k'ai, former commander-in-chief of the republican army. But Yüan, who still had military control of North China, declined to quit his power base to serve in Nanking. As the new President and would-be dictator, he revived Peking's capital status and allowed the boy-emperor to live on in the Forbidden City in only marginally reduced imperial style.

Two attempts were made to revive dynastic rule in Peking. In December, 1915, Yüan established himself as the first constitutional emperor of a new dynasty, the Hung-hsien (Grand Constitution). Military revolts compelled him to abandon the new dynasty after 83 days. Then, in 1917, following Yüan's death from unknown causes, a bizarre effort to restore the Ch'ing dynasty was engineered by Chang Hsun, who had been commander-in-chief of pro-Manchu forces in Nanking until the republican army drove him north in 1911. Chang was known as the Pig-Tailed General because he had always kept his Manchu-style queue to display his loyalty to the former regime, and his thousands of soldiers were commanded to do the same.

On July 1, the citizens of Peking awoke to an astonishing surprise: the flag of the hated Manchus was flying in the streets for the first time in five years, and the morning newspapers carried a bold announcement by the 11-year-old Emperor P'u-yi that he had been persuaded to return to the throne. It was a time of Boxer-style terror in the capital. Women were at the mercy of Chang's undisciplined troops; fear of persecution set off a stampede to the barber shops to buy false queues. Fortunately, the restoration lasted only 11 days. On July 7, a single republican plane flew over Peking to drop three small bombs on the Forbidden City—the first aerial bombardment in Chinese history. On July 12, northern warlords united to storm the city. The tyrannical Chang found sanctuary in the Dutch legation and his pig-tailed army either surrendered or fled, literally leaving a trail of tell-tale plaits behind them.

For another decade, disunity and grinding poverty continued to plague China while rival warlords wrestled for power and played military ping-pong over Peking. In this period the event of most lasting significance passed unobserved. In July, 1921, at a secret meeting held in Shanghai, the Chinese Communist Party was founded. Just 12 delegates attended, including the representative from Hunan province, Mao Tse-tung. At this point the Party had roughly 50 members. Two years later its strength was sufficient to induce Dr. Sun to invite Communists to join his Canton-based Nationalist (Kuomintang) organization as individual members.

The death of Dr. Sun Yat-sen—in Peking on March 12, 1925—spelled the virtual end of that uneasy alliance. It marked the beginning of ever-increasing rivalry between the two parties, leading to a complete split in 1927, when the new Nationalist leader, Chiang Kai-shek, launched a series of savage anti-Communist purges. The Nationalists now made Nanking their capital, and Peking was again called Pei'ping. Although the city was no longer the seat of imperial or political power, it was to suffer two more decades of conflict and confusion. From 1937 to 1945—throughout the course of the Sino-Japanese War—it remained under Japanese occupation; and the end of the Second World War marked only the resumption of civil war.

In 1918, Mao Tse-tung, aged 24, had lived briefly in Peking—working as an assistant librarian at the University and sharing a single room with seven other students from Hunan. On March 25, 1949, following the surrender of the Nationalist garrison, he returned to the city as the leader of a revolutionary force that had conquered China more completely than all the many different armies that had overwhelmed Peking in the past. Eight months later he proclaimed the birth of the People's Republic of China. "Our nation will never again be an insulted nation," he said on that occasion. "The Chinese have stood up." Pei'ping once again became Peking, the national capital. More importantly, for the first time in its history, it was the capital of a truly united China.

The Centre of the Earth

A ramp carved with writhing bas-relief dragons leads north towards the majestic Hall of Supreme Harmony (centre), where the Son of Heaven held audiences.

For more than 500 years, China was ruled from the Forbidden City—a cloistered, 250-acre complex of palaces, temples and ceremonial halls constructed in the centre of Peking by the 15th-Century Ming emperor, Yung-lo. Here, wrote a native philosopher, the emperor "stands in the centre of the earth and stabilizes the people within the four seas". Here, too, lived a retinue of thousands of concubines and eunuchs, some of them quick to take advantage of opportunities for intrigue or corruption; one eunuch official of the 16th Century managed to accumulate a huge fortune by abuse of his position. In 1912, the Chinese monarchy was finally stripped of its power, and the Forbidden City was opened to the public by the new republican regime. Today, renamed the Palace Museum, it is carefully preserved as a reminder of the excesses of the imperial past.

An archway forms the perfect frame for two entwined cypress trees.

A terrace lined with palms runs past pavilions once occupied by concubines. The only male attendants permitted to live in the Forbidden City were eunuchs.

Subdued light floods an elegant room in the residential quarters of the despotic Empress Dowager, Tz'u-hsi, who ruled China from 1861 until her death in 1908.

Golden dragons—the symbol of the emperor—perch on the roof of the Rain Flower Pavilion, a temple that once held Tibetan idols and erotic statuary.

A pavilion's eaves are lined with ceramic creatures from Chinese mythology.

Thrown into gloom by the afternoon sun, an alleyway separates the red walls of two palaces in the Forbidden City. The complex has 75 buildings in all.

At a gateway, a ferocious lion toys with a fretworked bauble.

A bronze elephant recalls the beasts used in state ceremonies.

Holding in its claws a flaming pearl—symbolic of the power and wisdom vested in the emperor—a magnificent dragon exhales stylized streams of smoke.

The Meridian Gate, the Forbidden City's southern entrance, looms over a snow-covered courtyard and the man-made meanders of the Golden Water River.

4

The Serious Business of Pleasure

Peking is sometimes portrayed abroad as a joyless city where millions of faceless workers spend their waking hours struggling to meet production targets and soaking up the latest political propaganda. Seen up close, however, the city reveals a capacity for relaxation and play that hardly meshes with such a grim portrait. Moreover, Peking possesses one dimension of pleasure—its cuisine—that can stand comparison with that of any metropolis in the world.

Admittedly, to Western eyes even leisure and recreation activities in Peking sometimes seem Orwellian. There is no mistaking, for example, the state's conviction that regular exercise makes for a stronger citizenry. Every morning and afternoon, Peking Radio broadcasts instructions for physical exercises, beginning with the exhortation: "Develop sporting activities! Defend the motherland!" Schools and factories and communes use loudspeakers to play their own such recordings during the stipulated recreation breaks. While these daily exercises are not compulsory, it is the recognized duty of *every* responsible citizen to keep himself healthy in body and mind, and anyone who neglects his exercises can expect to meet the disapproval of his peers. However, it would be wrong to explain so much collective exercise solely in terms of socio-political theory. The people of Peking tackle their favourite recreations with a genuine zest that transcends the demands of the state. Personal pride of achievement is also involved, a fact clearly indicated by the hordes of early risers who, entirely voluntarily and without supervision, gather in the parks at dawn to practise the balletic motions of various *wu shu*—traditional "war arts".

The attractive parklands of Peking are the focus of much of the citizenry's relaxation. There the people appear most at ease and carefree: families basking in the sunshine, buying ices and sweets and orangeade, and rowing in rented boats on the artificial lakes; children cavorting on winter ice or playing impromptu games of soccer; youths and adults flying home-made kites shaped like dragonflies or birds or bats; crowds milling around open-air concerts on special holidays; mothers watching their babes on swings and slides in the playgrounds.

Perhaps because television fare tends to be tediously propagandistic, the people of Peking have of necessity lost none of their facility for making their own entertainment. On the most simple level, one commonly sees men squatting in public places and sucking at long-stemmed, small-bowled brass pipes over a game of Chinese chess or checkers. Many play *p'ai-fen*, a card-game somewhat like bridge; more popular still is *p'u-k'e p'ai*—

Three members of the Inner Mongolian Equestrian Team gallop around the Temple of Heaven Park during the National Games, a one-to-two-week sports festival held every few years. The Mongolian displays include races, formation rides, such stunts as jumping through hoops of fire, and polo.

p'u-k'e being the Chinese pronunciation of "poker" and *p'ai* meaning "card". Gambling, of course, is outlawed in China, and the *p'u-k'e p'ai* players appear to have nothing more at stake than the satisfaction of winning. It is one of the few truly "bourgeois" pastimes to which the leadership raises no strong objection; the game of mah-jong, for example, which is still all the rage in Hong Kong and with Chinese communities abroad, is prohibited in China proper.

Young children in Peking also devote themselves to a rich assortment of games, including rope-skipping, the Chinese equivalent of hopscotch, and the ancient sport of collecting pet cicadas by using long sticks smeared with a sticky substance to pluck the noisy insects from trees. Most older children, however, have turned away from the more traditional pastimes and have whole-heartedly embraced a wide range of Western sports, from table-tennis and badminton to soccer and basketball.

Peking's facilities for these athletic imports are considerable. Many factories and schools now have well-equipped recreation halls. The Peking Workers' Stadium, completed in 1959 and occupying about 85 acres on the eastern fringe of the Imperial City, is China's largest sports complex, with an Olympic-sized track area, indoor and outdoor swimming pools and various ball-game courts. Near by stands the Peking Workers' Gymnasium, a towering, multi-windowed structure that ranks as the largest indoor athletics facility in the country. In addition, several parks have swimming pools, which immediately became highly popular after Mao Tse-tung's celebrated swim in the Yangtze in 1966.

Of the team sports, soccer is the favourite outdoor game—and appropriately so. According to some scholars, Chinese warriors—during the Han dynasty more than 2,000 years ago—started the game on its way with a fitness-training sport called *tsu-ch'iu* (kick-ball). Modern soccer was introduced to schools in Peking and other big cities in the mid-19th Century, but only since 1949 has it been played throughout China.

Nowadays the 80,000-seat Peking Workers' Stadium is filled to capacity for major inter-province matches or the visit of a team from abroad. The foreigners are usually opposed by a People's Liberation Army team called *Pa-i*, meaning "August 1"—an army holiday. Contrary to popular belief abroad, soccer and other Chinese sports are not without individual heroes. When the players are announced before the kick-off, a roar of appreciation greets the name of a star performer. But soccer in Peking is unusual in one particular respect—its lack of robust tackling and body-checking. "Friendship first, competition second," is the golden rule that has dominated all Chinese sport since the slogan was adopted at the time of the Sino-American "ping-pong diplomacy" in 1971, and it takes on special significance now in games that involve some physical contact.

In a way, the Chinese could be described as the most civilized sportsmen on earth. They encourage rival teams to train together before an

Seen from beneath a fringe of willow branches, weekend ice skaters—some of them with bicycles in tow—gather on a lake in Purple Bamboo Park, located in the north-west suburbs, to enjoy Peking's favourite winter sport.

important match at the stadium, and anything remotely approaching dangerous play is almost unknown. "Better to lose a point than injure an opponent," they say. Unfortunately, their gentle approach to football differs so markedly from that of other countries that it can defeat its own purpose of fostering friendship. For example, when *Pa-i* first played against New Zealand, the Peking crowd became angry at the visitors' hard-tackling, which was actually quite restrained by Western standards. Eventually, appeals for calm were relayed over the loudspeakers and the crowd was asked to enter into the right spirit of friendship. However, the spectators became even more incensed when New Zealand forwards harassed the Chinese goalkeeper as he carried the ball and sought room to kick it upfield. Another diplomatic announcement explained that such harassment was allowed under international rules, but the Peking fans continued to jeer at what they judged to be distinctly unfriendly play.

In terms of sporting recreation, the quality of life in Peking has indubitably been enriched in accordance with Mao Tse-tung's slogan: "Promote physical culture and build up the people's health." The late Chairman's influence on the artistic culture of the city—theatre, cinema, painting, music and literature—was no less great, but whether as a result these spheres have benefited is debatable, to say the least. Mao presented the Communist position on artistic expression very clearly as long ago as 1942, seven years before the triumph of the revolution and the advent of the People's Republic. At a party forum convened to discuss cultural matters, he said: "In the world today, all culture, all literature and art belong to definite classes and are geared to definite political lines. There is in fact

A left-handed batter in a woman's softball team awaits a pitch during a National Games contest. Baseball and this less demanding version of the game, introduced to China in the 1920s, have seen a recent surge in popularity—acknowledged in Peking by the building of a proper baseball stadium on a commune in the suburbs.

no such thing as art for art's sake, art that stands above the classes, art that is detached from or independent of politics. Proletarian literature and art are part of the whole proletarian revolutionary machine."

A quarter of a century later, that dogma was interpreted with irrational fanaticism during the Cultural Revolution. The arts became a prime target of ultra-left radicals who were waging their disorderly war—at Mao's behest—on "élitism", "revisionists" and "capitalist roaders". For a time, the campaign of so-called purification eliminated almost all forms of entertainment in Peking. Museums, theatres and cinemas closed down. Parks were open only intermittently. Almost every kind of foreign art and literature was outlawed. One decade later, in 1977, the Peking government lifted the ban on such masters of Western culture as Shakespeare and Cervantes, previously branded by the authorities as "feudal scribblers". But the effects of the Cultural Revolution on all Chinese arts were fundamental, and they persist.

Art, like everything else in China, must now clearly serve the people; that is to say, it should be expressed in terms that the masses can understand and appreciate fully, and it should deal with subjects relevant to the present-day needs and interests of the state. Inevitably, this has resulted in radical changes in all branches of the arts, and not least in that most popular form of Chinese theatre, the Peking Opera. Before the Cultural Revolution this classical combination of mime, music, singing, drama and acrobatics was predominantly a lavish display whose characters were emperors, concubines, ministers and generals living in imperial splendour. After the Opera's "purification" by ultra-leftists, its repertoire concentrated exclusively on revolutionary themes—a transformation supervised by Mao Tse-tung's wife, Chiang Ch'ing, who had been an actress in her younger days. The Chinese equivalent of Prince Charming was ousted as hero by the Patriotic Peasant; and the Cinderella-style heroine winning her way into court was replaced by a young girl in the People's Liberation Army overcoming the wiles of a capitalist landlord.

Some of the modern revolutionary operas have been so naïvely didactic in their story-line that a Western theatre-goer must be forgiven for imagining that he has attended an oriental version of the modern Theatre of the Absurd. An extreme example in the wake of the Cultural Revolution was an opera called *A Bucket of Dung*, in which the drama revolves around a man and his wife arguing interminably over a bucket of "night soil". She wants to give it to the commune to nourish the people's crops; he misguidedly wants to use it on his own private cabbage-patch. Naturally the wife wins the day, and the curtain falls on the triumphant scene of the couple scattering their faeces over communal pastures.

The other operas and ballets originally produced under Chiang Ch'ing's aegis number about a dozen. (To save the nation's face after Chiang Ch'ing was purged in 1976, the media announced that, insofar as they

were good productions, they were masterminded by Mao himself and not by his wife.) Of these, a production called "Taking Tiger Mountain by Strategy"—a tradition-rooted tale of a hero who braves snow and a very big tiger to invade a Nationalist stronghold—is the least likely to induce sleep. The most likely to have a soporific effect is "The Red Lantern"—a revision of what apparently was originally quite a good movie about resistance to the Japanese occupation of China.

My wife and I used to sit through these travesties of art because we imagined they would tell us something about the real state of mind of the Chinese people. In retrospect, I believe that the Chinese liked them little more than we did and only went to see them because hardly any other form of theatrical entertainment was available, or because the old-fashioned singing style and the acrobatic displays fascinated them. Since the purge, the "revolutionary" operas and ballets have been increasingly supplanted by more traditional productions, which attempt to show human beings as they really are rather than as mere political ciphers.

On a lighter entertainment level, Peking theatre offers two kinds of show. One is a straightforward variety concert comprising various acts— perhaps provincial acrobatic troupes, and some instrumentalists and vocalists. The other—far more popular—is a succession of verbal comedy acts, either monologues half-sung by a player to the rhythm of Chinese clappers (rather like castanets) or dialogues between two stand-up comics. Physically, the comedy teams are very much in the Laurel and Hardy tradition; the Chinese rely on body-shape to emphasize humour. But there all similarity ends. In Peking double-acts, the cross-chat is usually strongly political in content, and semi-satirical.

Immediately after Mao's death, for example, a major attraction at Peking's Bridge of Heaven Theatre was a series of propaganda concerts that extolled the virtues of Mao's successor, Chairman Hua, and poured scorn and hatred on the "radicals" who had sought in vain to achieve power. Of all the acts, by far the most popular with the public was a mocking mime of an "autopsy" being performed on Mao's widow, who allegedly was the leader of the treacherous group. The comedians rolled her imaginary body over with their feet and reported: "Behind Chiang Ch'ing's back there is a devil and on the back of her head there is another face." Then they mimed cutting open her stomach; and, to the delight of the audience, suddenly leaped back in horror on discovering that it was "seething with worms" and proceeded to cavort about the stage stamping on the invisible worms that had escaped.

In recent years, films have emerged as the most popular entertainment in Peking. Cinemas are scattered throughout the city, and more than a thousand film-showing teams are continually taking the latest state releases (about one new film a week) to communes, factories and schools. This art form, too, is geared to further the revolution. During my years in

Superskills in the Circus

One institution that has benefited exceptionally from the close supervision the Chinese government exercises over all aspects of culture is the Peking Circus. In late imperial times its performers were so little esteemed by the authorities that they carried the same yellow identity cards issued to prostitutes. Now they often boast the advantage of a childhood stint at one of several state-run Acrobatic Schools founded to encourage young gymnastic talent.

Their acts concentrate on skills, not thrills. Instead of emphasizing highwire routines or other daredevil feats, the members of the troupe—here seen at the Peking Stadium— offer virtuoso displays of balance, brawn and superb judgment that enthral the capacity audiences which they attract whenever they perform in the city. The only complaint is that such appearances are too infrequent: the Peking Circus spends much of its time on tour.

A team of trick cyclists achieves a fan-like effect descriptively entitled "The Peacock in His Pride".

A lithe strong-man uses neck, arm and leg muscles to demonstrate the art of simultaneously drawing four Tartar bows, noted for their lack of flexibility.

A sure-footed Cashmere goat inches its way towards the end of a tightrope after negotiating the obstacle of a vase placed in its path by an attendant.

Peking, there were no thrillers, comedies or romances as we know them. The unvarying theme was struggle by groups to make a better People's Republic, whether it involved peasants toiling to save their harvests, villagers seeking to overcome wicked landlords, industrial workers striving to increase production, soldiers battling against Nationalist "bandits", or children unmasking some "imperialist" saboteurs or spies.

Sports, theatre, cinema, art, literature—all have radically changed since the Communist revolution. Yet the greatest of all pleasures for the people of Peking remains basically unaltered. Throughout the ages they have attached an almost mystical importance to good cooking and eating, and their near-obsessive interest in food is no less striking today. In fact, it is virtually impossible to imagine a single day passing in Peking without some conversational reference to food.

Of course, as it did on everything else, the Cultural Revolution had its impact on Peking restaurants. Many of the more fashionable or luxurious eating-houses were temporarily closed down as being too "bourgeois" or "élitist"; and greater emphasis has been placed on so-called "masses' restaurants" where everyone can eat at reasonable cost in strictly informal surroundings. But let no one imagine that Communism has weaned the Chinese people away from their millennia-old conviction about the virtue of good nutrition inventively created. In Peking you can still enjoy just about the best Chinese food in the world. And as a gastronomic capital, Peking is still rivalled only by a few other cities, such as Paris and New York. This seems particularly impressive when one considers that all restaurants are state-run and that their employees receive the job by assignment.

In many ways, a meal at a good Peking restaurant is like a well-structured Chinese poem. It should number between eight and 12 courses, thus echoing the strophes of certain classical forms of Chinese poetry; and each dish—in colour, texture, nutritional characteristics and flavour—should set off those immediately preceding it and following it. Moreover, any menu worth its salt will be written in elegant calligraphy, and the names of dishes tend more towards the poetic than to the descriptive—"lotus shark's fin", "squirrel fish", and so on.

We are, of course, talking of high-class Chinese food. For most Peking citizens the main meal of the day—taken at midday—usually means no more than rice and a simple side dish of meat or vegetables. Nevertheless, enthusiasm and care is brought to the preparation of food for all tables, no matter how humble. And, at all levels of cuisine, the Chinese ideal remains the same: to consume food through the mouth in much the same spirit as poetry is consumed by the mind.

The earliest recorded Chinese poetry, dating from about 1000 B.C., conveys a sense of man as a kind of privileged guest in a natural world incredibly rich in vegetation and wildlife. At the time, the Chinese people were concentrated in the fertile region of the Yellow River valley. Later, as the population expanded over a vast territory, much of the wildlife was destroyed. Famine arose from natural disasters—drought, floods, earthquakes—and, just as often, from wars and maladministration. But these misfortunes served only to encourage still greater ingenuity in devising new dishes to reap maximum benefit, with minimum waste, from the little they had. Not only did it breed in the Chinese a profound respect for food, it also resulted in a range of regional cuisines that no other country—with the exception of France—can match in terms of richness and variety. This regional diversity is splendidly represented in the restaurants of Peking.

Traditionally, the Chinese divide foods into two basic categories—those that "heat" the human system and those that "cool" it. Obviously, chilli peppers are warming and almond custard is cooling, but the Chinese extend this division to all foodstuffs in a way Westerners find pedantic or irrelevant. They also have an unusual dietary theory. In the West, doctors mostly recommend high-protein, low-carbohydrate diets for those wishing to lose weight. But the Chinese think this is illogical; they consider that high-protein foods, being the richest and the most expensive, are sure to make you fat. Almost to a man, they consider it incomprehensible to eat any meal at all without a hearty portion of rice, noodles or other form of carbohydrate, and they have no particular belief that sugar is fattening. If anyone thinks this is foolish, let them look around Peking: living on a grain-based diet, the people are sturdy and well-built, and you rarely see obesity. Do the Chinese as a race differ subtly in physiology and metabolism? Perhaps. Certainly a Chinese person who goes over to an American-style high-protein diet may quickly begin to look flabby.

The only time I had serious doubts about the Chinese nutritional theory was when a skinny and rather unpleasant official in the Peking Foreign Ministry told me (for the umpteenth time): "Ah, I see you have put on weight." At the time I had been on a crash diet and had succeeded in losing almost 20 pounds. I told him rather sharply that he was talking nonsense. He looked me up and down once again. "In that case," he said, "you must have grown shorter."

Theory be damned—there is no way to lose weight in Peking if you eat out regularly in Chinese restaurants; and a foreigner can hardly avoid eating out since it represents one of the city's chief forms of entertainment. So I propose to recall a few lyrical moments in Peking's top restaurants, and let the waistline take care of itself.

Before doing so, however, let me hasten to add that the phrase "top restaurants" has nothing to do with the decor. Most Peking restaurants are dreary in appearance, often ill-heated in winter and lacking air-conditioning in summer. But you go there strictly to eat, not to flirt or admire the wallpaper; and only the most narrow-minded or ascetic person will come away unimpressed by the food.

In an opera entitled "The Red Detachment of Women", revolver-wielding female warriors, appropriately lighted, strike a pose vibrant with revolutionary fervour.

One should not expect to dine on the kind of adulterated food offered in most so-called Chinese restaurants in the West. An essential characteristic of true Chinese food is that it is served in small pieces (only in Inner Mongolia have I seen a Chinese dish with a portion of meat so big that it needed a knife to be eaten). Knives are reserved for use in the kitchen or at a side-table, as for instance in the slicing of Peking Duck. This leads to some anomalies. For example, the Chinese sometimes serve pieces of chicken or duck in which the bone has been cut clean through or shattered by beating; the customer may need to gnaw at it while holding it in his chopsticks and then spit out any bits of bone that get into his mouth. The Chinese also eschew the use of fish-knives. They fully expect to get a mouthful of fish-bones when eating, and again they spit them out either on the floor or in a pile, on the tablecloth, if there is one.

Another notable characteristic of Chinese cooking is that it is economical. It concentrates on frying (both stir-frying and deep-frying) more than on boiling and grilling processes, which tend to waste some of the nutritional material. Some foods are, of course, boiled; but in circumstances when a temperature of 212°F. is regarded as ideal for the cooking process, the Chinese often prefer to steam the food so that nothing is lost.

Few people in China like to eat or drink dairy products. Indeed, the majority of Chinese consider dairy products just as disgusting as we might consider the eating of a duck's brain or the flesh of a dog. In Inner Mongolia, in Tibet and Central Asia, the Chinese have learned from the indigenous people to tolerate and even appreciate milk—both fresh and fermented—as well as hard cheese and other products of the mammary glands of goats, yaks, camels, horses and sometimes cows. But in Peking— itself on the fringe of Mongolia—cow's milk is regarded mainly as a food for babies whose mothers do not have enough of their own. As for the smell of cheese or even butter on a foreigner's breath, it is as revolting to the local people as the smell of garlic is to many Englishmen. (Incidentally, if you don't like the smell of garlic, don't get on a Peking bus.)

All this just goes to show how relative our concepts of nutrition are. A host of race-relations problems can be determined by the smell of different foodstuffs and by prejudices about what is and is not fit for human consumption. I sometimes almost wanted to strangle my driver in Peking because he ate so much garlic and because he smeared himself with an ointment for rheumatism that smelled like rotting toads. But he probably thought I smelled disgusting after a lunch of lamb-chops, cheese and wine.

But I'm straying from the main arena—the restaurants themselves. Many people think the best restaurant in Peking is the Ch'eng-tu, which specializes in the spicy cuisine of Szechwan province. This establishment in the southern part of the city is particularly appealing because it occupies an old Chinese mansion with tiled roofs and painted ceilings—once a residence, it is believed, of Yüan Shih-kai, the pseudo-Republican usurper who overthrew the Ch'ing dynasty in 1911. Entering via a green-shaded outer courtyard, you are guided by waitresses in white tunics to one of several dining-rooms located around the inner, interlocking courtyards. The whole place exudes traditional China, and so its customers—mostly foreigners or Chinese officials entertaining overseas visitors—are prepared to pay the rather high prices demanded for the restaurant's admittedly exquisite food. (At one time, farewell banquets for departing diplomats were thrown at the Ch'eng-tu by a Peking Foreign Ministry official named Mr. Tu Kuo-wei. Awkwardly, his Chinese name, when spoken, sounded to the English ear exactly like "Do Go Away".)

I found it advisable to visit the Ch'eng-tu in advance and go over the menu with the head-waiter before bringing one's guests. Left to arrange the menu themselves, the management would pad it with expensive dishes ("silver-ear" fungus, for example, which looks like pieces of a white bath sponge and tastes of hardly anything) to the detriment of the Szechwan dishes. At the Ch'eng-tu, they displayed mild irritation at a foreigner specifying his own menu, but they did begrudgingly accept it as his right.

For starters, they offered specially pickled eggs which—unlike the brownish-black "aged" eggs served at most Peking restaurants—came out white and orange. They looked like fresh hard-boiled eggs but, in fact, the pickling process—a matter of boiling them in tea or other liquids for several hours—made their texture soft and sticky. The eggy flavour was emphasized, but not at all in an offensive way. Still more strange to the Western palate was the cheesy-style of Szechwan bean-curd, with its sharp savoury flavour; and the *pièce de résistance* of their "cold dishes" was a plate of sliced chicken served with a blistering black pepper sauce.

Practically no Szechwan meal is complete without the famous *kan pien niu-jou ssu*—dried strips of beef fried up with hot peppers, carrots and celery; and if this doesn't take the roof off your mouth, you can always follow up with *ma-la tou-fu*—bean-curd cubes in a hot pepper meat gravy, somewhat Mexican in character, and one of the best things in a Peking restaurant. Not all Szechwan food is hot, however. One of the finest un-peppered specialities is *chang ch'a ya-tzu*—duck boiled in tea and smoked in camphor-wood chips. The boiling in tea removes much of the fat, while the smoking bestows an indescribably delicate flavour.

Many Americans and Europeans know Szechwan food quite well from restaurants in their own countries, but they are less familiar with the more subtle Yunnan style of cooking from the far south-west of China. In Peking I was introduced to this cuisine at a little place called K'ang Lo (Healthy and Happy) on upper Wang Fu Ching avenue. Here they served a famous concoction known as *t'ao-hua fan* (peach-flower rice) which is made by boiling rice so long that the water evaporates and the rice begins to cling to the sides of the saucepan, going crisp and scorching itself into a delicate pinkish-brown colour. The hot rice is scraped off and put on a serving dish.

Diners enjoy a relaxed lunch at one of Peking's most acclaimed restaurants, the Ch'eng-tu, which specializes in highly spiced recipes from Szechwan province.

Savouring the do-it-yourself delights of the Mongolian dish of "shua yang jou", clients of a downtown restaurant dip strips of mutton in boiling water to cook.

Then a sizzling bowl of sweet-and-sour sauce, with prawns and chopped vegetables, is poured over the rice with a great whooshing sound.

Another popular Yunnan speciality—one of the simplest but most charming—is *kuo-ch'iao mien* (crossing-the-bridge noodles), which consists of nothing more than noodles in a strong chicken broth. The K'ang Lo headwaiter, a plump and amiable fellow, liked to tell customers how the dish got its peculiar name. According to him, there was once a young Chinese scholar studying hard to enter the imperial service and restore the faded fortunes of his family. Finding his parents' house too noisy, he took his books to a pavilion situated at the end of a long garden, beyond an ornamental brook crossed by a small hump-backed bridge. Servants brought him meals in the pavilion, but then he complained that the food was always cold by the time it arrived. So they dreamed up a dish of chicken broth—crossing-the-bridge noodles—which would have just enough fat floating on top to insulate the heat inside and keep the noodles warm until they reached the hungry scholar.

There are many other stories about the origin of this dish. But perhaps the simplest of explanations is the most plausible: when pulled out of the bowl with chopsticks, the long noodles remind people of the chain-suspension bridges that are common in the gorges of south-west China.

By this time, you may be wondering whatever happened to the famous Peking Duck. Please do not get the impression that I despise or dislike it. Quite the contrary. It is without doubt one of the world's great culinary creations, but it is so well-known abroad that I would merely like to correct a few wrong notions about the dish rather than describe it in detail. First, several fallacies surround the manner of serving trimmings for Peking Duck. The proper presentation has it accompanied by unleavened flour pancakes of almost paper-thinness. The duck slices are then dipped in brown sauce and wrapped in the pancakes with fresh spring onions, and the resulting greasy and dripping cylinder of duck-filled dough can be eaten with the fingers or with chopsticks, as one prefers. The sauce should be made from a fermentation of the same dough used to make the pancakes. It is not sweet and, contrary to common practice in southern China, it is not made from plums or any other fruit; the fermentation process supplies the flavour. Nor is it the custom in Peking to swell the garnishings with the raw strips of cucumber or green beet that are served with "Peking Duck" in Hong Kong and elsewhere.

The trouble with this dish in Peking is that you may be expected to eat virtually every part of the bird. The Chinese consider the three best parts to be the thin strip of flesh along the backbone, the fatty tail, and the split head (from which only the tiny brain is eaten). It is a compliment to be offered these morsels, and it is slightly bad manners to refuse them, although the Chinese recognize that some people cannot bring themselves to poke around in the brain, with the roasted eye staring glumly out from

In the kitchen of a city-centre restaurant where the speciality is Peking Duck, birds hang suspended on hooks and roast over an open wood fire. The ducks have been force-fed a doughy mixture of flour, sorghum grain, maize and soyabean cake to give them the plumpness and tenderness that gourmets require.

the other side. But I myself can see no charm in consuming all these unpleasant parts of the duck before getting down to the delicious deep-fried liver, and the crisp skin and meat.

It is impossible to describe in detail here all the many succulent dishes I enjoyed in Peking. I will conclude with the dish that merits very special attention: *shua yang-jou*, variously translated as "rinsed mutton", "Mongolian hot-pot" or (most accurately) "scalded mutton". This is, for me, the very best dish to be had in Peking. At least twice a month in winter, I tried to go to the Nationalities Restaurant, just off Wang Fu Ching, where it was prepared to its ultimate perfection. This restaurant was notable, too, for the extreme friendliness of the staff, and, most important, its management was efficient in taking orders at short notice over the telephone.

Curiously, many Peking citizens have difficulty in accepting the existence of a stranger (especially an unknown foreigner) who is only a voice on the telephone. Therefore, when organizing a dinner party, it is necessary to visit a good Peking restaurant in advance not only to discuss the menu, but also to convince the management that you really do exist. In the case of the Nationalities Restaurant, however, I had only to pick up the telephone in our apartment and say "English journalist" (the Chinese usually do not distinguish between "English" and "British"). The person on the other end would then reply with the Peking equivalent of "yeah", which—pronounced with the correct Chinese intonation—sounds something like "wuah" and signifies: "I think I recognize your voice and know who you are." Then all I had to say was: "Monday, 7 p.m., six people, cold plate and scalded mutton, lamb's tail dessert, usual price, thanks, bye." "Wuah."

But to return to Peking's finest fare, *shua yang-jou*, the philosophy of this dish is simple enough—but the execution has to be perfect. First, a fine cut of lamb or mutton is chilled almost to freezing point, then cut into paper-thin slices by butchers so crafty that one suspects them of having practised tantric breathing exercises in the course of their apprenticeship. These strips are arranged in a precise circle and presented on plain white china plates—as many plates of meat as the diners require. Meanwhile, a few preliminary courses are to be savoured.

Having whetted their appetites with candied walnuts, carefully matured eggs, ribbons of jellyfish flesh, and small pieces of mandarin orange, gastronomes can go on to eat shark's fin in a sauce of egg-white so light that it almost flies away; and, if they are hearty eaters, they may also have some fried chicken pieces with especially hot red and green peppers. I advise no one to eat anything else before the central dish. Chinese hosts usually feel it obligatory to add some shashliks—minced lamb with sesame seeds cooked over charcoal on skewers—but this is really misguided hospitality, since it jades the appetite for what is to follow.

Now one gets down to the real pleasure of the evening. Placed on the table is a beautiful copper pot consisting of a charcoal brazier and a doughnut-shaped scalding pan. The pan is full of water and is centred

At an agricultural commune within the Peking city limits, workers wind rice noodles into bundles for easy storage and transport. Noodles, made from wheat as well as rice or bean starch, are a basic element of Chinese cuisine.

beneath a foot-high funnel that carries the charcoal fumes upwards. On top of the funnel is the key to the whole affair: a plain metal disc which controls, with incredible accuracy, the speed at which the charcoal burns and therefore the boiling of the water in the receptacle above.

Together with the strips of raw lamb or mutton comes a clearly defined and essential set of accompaniments. There are: unleavened wholemeal rolls covered in sesame seed; plates of raw onion and coriander-leaf, chopped small; sweet-pickled garlic cloves; and a tray (looking for all the world like an artist's palette) of eight different sauces—soya, Chinese vinegar, chilli, pink bean-curd paste, fermented fish extract, liquefied sesame, rice-wine, and a green mush made from some kind of Chinese leek that I have never succeeded in identifying. The waiter carefully mixes these colourful sauces, then pours the mixture into small individual bowls.

After munching some pickled garlic, the diners plunge their chopsticks into the plates of delicate raw mutton and dip the slices in the boiling water of the brazier. If the temperature is right, the mutton should be well cooked in substantially less than a minute; and because the chopsticks are sterilized every time they are immersed in the water, nobody should worry about taking meat from the same pot as everyone else. The cooked meat-strips are then dipped into the individual bowls of sauce—partly to flavour them, partly to cool them—and some of the chopped onion and coriander-leaf should be picked up on the way. A bite of sesame roll—and the meal is begun in earnest.

After a short while, the waiters bring fresh cabbage leaves, *chiao-tzu* (Chinese ravioli), and two types of noodle—one made from wheat-flour, the other from rice-flour. I recommend introducing the cabbage at an early stage, but not drowning the mutton immediately in *chiao-tzu* and noodles. In fact, I prefer to leave out the semi-transparent rice-flour noodles altogether, because they are virtually flavourless and simply impede the enjoyment of the other ingredients. Finally, after the *shua yang-jou*, there should be enough sauce left to bear dilution with the consommé that has been quietly brewing from the ingredients in the brazier-pot. It is not a strong soup—indeed, without the remnants of mixed sauce, it is insipid. Add the sauce, however, and you have a savoury nectar which can be drunk straight from the sauce-bowl—and which perfectly settles the digestion at the end of one of the world's great gastronomic experiences.

Citizens in Training

Heading towards their homes at the end of an eight-hour schoolday, two girls pause to navigate a deep puddle that has been left by a late-summer downpour.

Growing up in Peking is an earnest affair in which the joys of childhood are tempered by a government-instilled spirit of high purpose—summed up in the oft-repeated saying that "children are the successors to the revolution". From kindergarten on, youngsters are taught to help each other and serve society with selfless zeal. School plays, songs and recitations endlessly reiterate the ideals of the state, and political virtue is further maintained by sessions in which pupils criticize themselves and their classmates. Above all, the importance of productive labour is always kept in view. Not only do older students have to put in yearly service on communes or in factories, but even the youngest schoolgoers must practise manual skills—such as sorting or packaging light-industry products—to appreciate better the varied aspects of a useful working life.

Hands linked to prevent any straying from the fold, toddlers are led to a neighbourhood kindergarten by the mother of one member of the troupe. Most mothers in Peking work, and factories often provide nursery facilities for children who are too young to go to school.

Beneath a poster of children wearing national minority costumes, kindergarten pupils act out a parable about the come-uppance of a lazy, anti-social rabbit.

Military pride is cultivated in children from an early age. Above, youngsters in a primary school enact a battle scene that glorifies the exploits of the Chinese navy. At left, a small boy proudly wears the uniform of a soldier in the People's Liberation Army—a prestigious career sought by millions of volunteers when they reach 18.

Under their school banner, shovel-toting students trek into the country to work on a commune and fulfil the Maoist aim of learning from practical experience.

5

Consumerism on a Close Rein

Foreigners who go to Peking these days are often so bedazzled by the opportunity of seeing this long-closed world that they tend to style themselves as instant experts. As a result, an overseas resident of the city often has to listen to an excited recital of the impressions of someone who has been in China fully two or three days. It is one of the hazards of living there, and old hands usually take it with a resigned and faintly amused air of "Here we go again". There is, however, one matter on which even the most self-involved visitors will eagerly seek advice: where to shop and what to buy. Newcomers sense that Peking has some unique shopping experiences to bestow—and that feeling is not mistaken.

Even a single shopping expedition can be fascinating to a Westerner, for this is a world without credit cards, discounts, price-cutting, equipment rentals, trading stamps—and with a minimum of advertising. And for those who stay in Peking for an appreciable length of time, shops and markets can provide a true treasury of information. To see the goods on display, to note prices and observe what people buy, gives an insight into the life of China's common man, his standard of living and his everyday priorities. It also gives one a better understanding of the way the country is run.

In Peking, you can forget about shopping around for the best prices on any given product. All prices are determined by the state; and even in the open-air food markets there is no haggling over the cost of a chicken or a pound of persimmons. The price is the price—and it will be the same at every other market. This does not mean, however, that you will want to buy indiscriminatively or off-the-cuff. For the foreigner there are still some tremendous values to be had in Peking: modern printed silks that are less expensive than anywhere else in the world; beautiful old embroidered fabrics; superb replicas of ancient ceramic and pottery figures; old furniture and curios. But in all things, bargaining is positively futile.

In the provinces there have been instances of spontaneous marketing of foodstuffs by the peasants, who do sometimes fix their own prices and even bargain with the shopper; such occurrences are frowned on, but they still take place. To my knowledge, such entrepreneurial behaviour never happens in Peking. The difference between Peking and the provinces is characteristic of many spheres of Chinese life. The authorities like this city to be a model, both for Chinese from other parts of the country and for foreigners who live or visit there and form most of their impressions about China from the capital. Peking thus adheres to the highest standards in retailing methods. Prices do fluctuate, but only according to the dictates

Beneath a sign urging them to help develop the national economy, customers throng a hardware counter at the Hsin-hsin, a department store in Peking's Ch'ien Men district. The government-run emporium is chiefly known for its clothes: fashion-conscious shoppers go there to inspect the latest designs and fabrics from Shanghai, China's sartorial centre.

of the state. Such rigid control reduces hoarding and profiteering in times of shortages; equally important, it allows the standard cost of perishable foodstuffs to be changed when there is a glut on the market or vice-versa.

When I arrived in Peking, I was astounded to see how well a Communist economy could satisfy fundamental consumer needs. Basic foods—fresh fruit, meat and vegetables—were invariably plentiful and relatively low-priced. I saw few real luxuries and those were mostly aimed at foreign customers. But luxury is a relative concept; goods such as sweets and liquors—quite ordinary perhaps to an American or a European—are regarded as luxuries by the citizens of Peking. Most of these people will never be able to afford anything more expensive than a bicycle and a sewing-machine, an electric fan or perhaps a camera. However, they definitely have money to indulge themselves occasionally with preserved foods, woollen garments or toys for the children. And in terms of essentials for everyday living, there are no really serious shortages.

The situation in Peking contrasts markedly with that in Moscow, where I lived for three years prior to my transfer to China. In the Soviet Union, I found that prices were generally high in relation to incomes, and shortages of the most elementary goods—such as kettles, toothbrushes and soap—were so endemic that they were accepted as a matter of course. Why isn't this so in Peking? The most significant factor in what I call China's "austere consumerism" has been the Party's decision to emphasize production of agricultural and light industrial goods as the fundamental contribution to the people's welfare and as the most important incentive to the building up of a better economic base. The result is the great paradox of Peking: a consumer society operating effectively on extremely low incomes.

Of course, when relating Peking prices to incomes, one must always bear in mind that the Chinese mostly pay very little rent or none at all, and that they are unburdened by income tax, mortgages or car ownership. Education is universal, compulsory and free, except for some textbooks that have to be bought by the student himself. And the various co-operative medical schemes operated by factories and communes mean that routine hospital treatment comes cheap. Thus, if we take a fairly average Peking couple—each earning, say, 60 yuan (about $32) a month—their monthly budget of 120 yuan might break down as follows: 65 yuan for food; 3 yuan as rent for their small two-room or, perhaps, three-room apartment; 3 yuan for bus fares; 2.60 yuan for electricity and gas; 0.30 yuan for water; and 3.50 yuan for day-nursery. This leaves them 42.60 yuan a month for clothing, theatre or cinema, beer and cigarettes, dining out or whatever. They do not have such amenities as a washing machine or a private telephone. But their basic needs are comfortably met, and they can put aside a few yuan each month in a modest bank deposit account earning them about 3 per cent interest.

Now let us visit the Peking shops and see what their money can buy.

Near a venerable gateway in north-east Peking, an open-air stall displays cabbages and onions from a local commune. Since few Peking citizens own refrigerators, they buy only enough perishable items to satisfy daily needs.

A convenient and interesting shopping venue for the newcomer to Peking is Wang Fu Ching, known during the Cultural Revolution as People's Street, and known to foreigners a few decades ago as Morrison Street, in memory of a celebrated Peking correspondent of *The Times* of London. Today, no one calls it by anything but its ancient name of Wang Fu Ching, meaning "Well of the Princes' Residences" and recalling that imperial princes once lived in the area and had their water drawn from the local well. (The well is now buried beneath the offices of the *People's Daily*, China's leading national newspaper, with a four-million-plus- circulation.)

Wang Fu Ching begins a short step from the 17-storey Peking Hotel and runs due north, a few blocks east of the old Forbidden City. It is no Tokyo Ginza, no Regent Street and certainly no Fifth Avenue; indeed, it is such a narrow main thoroughfare that cyclists have been banned from it because they were congesting traffic. Nevertheless, it is Peking's most prestigious shopping area, lined with stores selling the most sophisticated goods to be found in the capital.

On Wang Fu Ching, my first stop used to be at the Hsin-hua (New China) Bookstore, the main shop of the organization that monopolizes all retail book outlets in Peking. It is an echoing, ill-lit emporium. Soldiers and students cluster near the entrance and glance through the latest political pamphlets or jostle around the section selling sheet music of up-lifting revolutionary songs and the piano scores of modern revolutionary operas and ballets. Upstairs, in a reading room reserved for children, a few dozen teenagers sit in rows, soaking up the currently orthodox works of fiction or general knowledge. The shelves display an overwhelming predominance of technical and scientific books, dealing with everything from abortion to geology. Prices are relatively low—ranging from less than 1 yuan to about 5 yuan (about 50 cents to 3 dollars)—and yet I notice that most customers are content to linger in the store, reading hard and then leaving without buying.

Even if one couldn't read Chinese, this bookstore would be of some interest, since there are so many illustrated works. One especially popular section is devoted to pocket-sized comics, all of a political or educational nature. The comics depicting foreigners are mildly amusing and revealing, although it is a shade disturbing to see some of the cliché prototypes being fed to young minds in Peking: big-nosed American G.I.s, European nuns maltreating Chinese children, and gangster-like Soviet spies. The only foreigners I have seen glorified in the comics are Norman Bethune, a Canadian doctor who died in 1939 while serving with the Red Army as a surgeon and who is proclaimed as a model of socialist internationalism; author Maxim Gorky, whom the Chinese seem to regard roughly as the Russian equivalent of their own Lu Hsun, a novelist much quoted as a supporter of Communism; and of course, Marx, Engels and Lenin.

Across the street from the Hsin-hua Bookstore is the true focal point of Peking's shopping world: the Pai Huo Ta Lou (Hundred Goods Emporium), a three-storey department store that offers virtually everything the ordinary citizen can buy, except fresh foodstuffs and medicines. The store itself is a grimy and rather gloomy place, stuffy in summer, freezing in winter, with a dirty stone floor that is dotted with sputum all the year round. It is, however, the biggest and best known store in the capital city, serving an estimated 100,000 customers between 8.30 a.m. and 8.30 p.m. each day. Interestingly, a fleet of military staff cars is almost always seen parked near the entrance: evidently, the officers of the regiments around Peking like to do their shopping there.

Like other shops in Peking, the Hundred Goods Emporium is always busy—another proof of the state's well-planned retailing policy. The shoppers—at least as many men as there are women—look reasonably well-fed and cheerful, but they buy cautiously, and their arms are not full of bulging carrier-bags when they leave. Near the entrance, soldiers and civilians are milling around a counter that displays special preserves, chocolates, candy, wines and cigarettes. There is unusual interest today because some high-class cigarettes, normally kept for export, have become available. Yet few people scramble to get to the front. Most customers quietly form their own queue—of insignificant length compared with the interminable lines I have seen formed in similar circumstances in Moscow. Moreover, the shop assistants display none of that special brand of

A customer selects a cut of meat sliced from the carcasses hanging in a butcher's shop on Tung Tan street. Most families regularly eat pork, which is plentiful, but cereals still make up three-quarters of the typical Peking diet.

arrogance and indolence that characterizes their Russian counterparts. They have a job that carries little prestige; they enjoy no bonus geared to the volume of sales, and no overtime pay. Yet they work hard and conscientiously, and calm and order usually prevail.

The demand for cigarettes at this counter reminds me of a widespread weakness I have already noticed on the streets: the vast majority of men in Peking are heavy smokers. Few women smoke and the habit is slightly discouraged for young men. Yet, in general, there has never been any serious effort to discourage smoking for health reasons. Cigarette packs are still sold without any warning notice or information about tar content. Chairman Mao was himself a heavy smoker until near the end of his life. But I have no explanation for the casual acceptance of this addiction in a society that has otherwise campaigned so vigorously and effectively for clean living (hard drugs, alcoholism and venereal disease have virtually been eliminated in the People's Republic).

In contrast to the cigarette counter, another section of the Pai Huo Ta Lou is doing a brisk trade in two simple objects that have probably contributed more to Peking's public health than anything else, excepting, of course, the city's hospital service. They are selling enamel basins and large vacuum flasks. Almost no-one in Peking except foreigners and top political leaders has a private bath or shower, but the people are becoming more hygiene-conscious, and the enamel basin enables them to wash regularly. Since running hot water is not provided to the vast mass of the population, water is boiled on the stove. Whatever is not used is kept hot in the flask for washing up or for drinking later on.

The sides of these basins and flasks are decorated with all the officially sponsored art themes that are in vogue. Pandas, bamboos and flowers have been favourite motifs. There is also a strong line in political heroics: sturdy workers and peasants toiling in factory and field, brave militia girls guarding the coasts, ballerinas in famous and often subliminally erotic revolutionary poses. Perhaps these themes are dismally the same, but it occurs to me that they are certainly no more offensive than the many shoddy styles of decor to be found on mass-produced goods in Western stores. Certainly, the shoppers appear to like them.

Over at the cosmetics counter, the range of goods is strikingly limited in some respects. There are plenty of shampoos and a goodly selection of facial creams, which sell especially well during the cold, dry winters. But there are no strictly artificial beauty aids such as lipsticks and mascara. The near-by music counter has an enormous variety of simple instruments, including the *p'i p'a*, a string instrument of central Asian origin, and a twisted confusion of Pan-pipes called the *sheng*. And the liquor counter features a wide range of wines, one of the most expensive being ginseng wine, which costs about 6 yuan a bottle (just over $3); its former reputation as an aphrodisiac has faded, but it is still said to give vitality. There are also

A cobbler awaits clients at his pavement premises in north Peking. Only a few such private businesses—simple repair services run by old people—still exist.

heavy red wines, locally made whiskey, vodka and gin, and the much sought-after *mao t'ai*—a colourless, 80° proof spirit made from sorghum.

To the rear of the store's ground floor is the electrical goods department —a section of special interest because it tells us much about China's production of relatively expensive consumer goods, and much about what the people of Peking can—or cannot—afford to buy. Here one finds a narrow range of expensive clocks, irons, fans, heaters and other labour-saving devices. There are also several models of television sets and an enormous selection of transistor radios. Television sets and radios are mass-produced in China, because through these media the government can keep in constant touch with the entire population, issuing its directions and exhortations, and broadcasting strictly controlled news programmes.

A television set is a luxury item; even an 8-inch black-and-white set costs about half-a-year's wages for an average worker. The great majority have no set of their own and must watch television in institutional surroundings —on sets owned by communes, factories, schools and community social centres. Chinese-made transistor radios, on the other hand, are ubiquitous. One particular model—called "The East is Red"—sells for a mere 19 yuan.

Predictably, radio programming is considerably more extensive than television fare. The Central China Broadcasting station, located in Peking, transmits three radio programmes simultaneously for a total air-time of 47 hours a day. One group of programmes consists of news and news commentaries, and the other two provide music and other cultural fare.

Walking upstairs to the first floor of the Hundred Goods Emporium (there are no elevators), one encounters a major difference between the display of a Peking store and its Western counterpart. Here they sell clothes and—for those who make their own garments—a variety of fabrics. Although the array of silks is impressive, the section as a whole has nothing like the range in fashions one is accustomed to seeing in a big Western city store. To be sure, there are attractive dresses and play-suits for children in a riot of different colours, an assortment of patterned skirts and blouses for women, and for both sexes some fairly stylish padded overcoats with fur or artificial collars. But, in general, *de rigueur* dress for adults remains the same: baggy trousers and open-neck shirts or blouses in summer, and padded tunics of subdued blue, brown, grey and green shades in winter. The tunics range in price from 5.50 yuan to 11 yuan, depending on the quality of the material. Trousers cost from 5 yuan to about 9 yuan. The most popular footwear—made of rubber-soled canvas—are 3 yuan and upwards. Leather shoes are expensive at 10 yuan and more.

Most of the clothes are of cotton, and there is a limit on how much an individual can buy. In 1954, responding to nationwide clothing shortage, the authorities introduced cotton rationing. Each person was allowed an annual ration of three yards of the material—a figure that had nearly tripled by the mid-1970s. The workings of the rationing system are simple:

A State-sanctioned Indulgence

Peking is remarkably short of public vices, but cigarette smoking is a conspicuous exception to the general rule. Many citizens of Peking are heavy smokers and a wide variety of colourfully packeted brands cater to the habit. The packages are usually labelled both in traditional Chinese characters and in *p'in yin*, an alphabetical system of lettering that is being introduced by the authorities to promote common pronunciation of words throughout the country. Some brands also bear English names, since the export of cigarettes to Hong Kong and other destinations where English is a *lingua franca* is a valuable source of foreign currency.

The home market is even more lucrative: China is the world's second largest tobacco producer, after the United States, and the immense revenues to the government gained from the domestic sale of cigarettes (average local price: 15 U.S. cents for 20) may be the main reason why the state has yet to launch a serious anti-smoking campaign.

citizens are issued coupons for the prevailing allowance figure; the stores, in turn, mark all garments according to the amount of cotton used in their manufacture; when purchasing clothes, the buyer hands over his money and coupons, and receives change for both.

Woollen fabrics have remained unrationed, as have the products of China's fast-expanding artificial-fibre industry (Peking is a manufacturing centre for nylon and polyester, as well as other textiles). Apart from cotton, textile supplies seem easily able to keep up with demand. Peking people, I have observed, are much less inclined to spend money on clothes than, for instance, Muscovites, who are positively clothes-crazy.

Any Westerner is bound to be struck by some of the deficiencies of goods in Peking. For example, when my wife and I arrived in Peking, Judy wanted a vacuum cleaner—which, hitherto, she had regarded as an essential non-luxury household item. But there weren't any at all in the Hundred Goods Emporium. We therefore sought the generous help of Comrade Li, the driver of the Shanghai automobile we had rented from the Capital Car Hire Company. He combed the city to find us a reasonably priced vacuum cleaner. Ultimately he bluffed his way into a store that sold exclusively to government officials and persuaded the management to part with one of their precious suction machines in the interest of international friendship. They did so unwillingly—and I only wish they had been more unwilling.

The Chinese vacuum cleaner cost us 250 yuan. Li was delighted at his success and he kept telling us that it was "very good for cleaning carpets". What he actually meant was that it was a good deal better than the short-handled sorghum-twig brooms used in most Peking households. And even that judgment was questionable. The device had every fault imaginable. The filter was attached to the dust-bag by a piece of flimsy tape that was almost impossible to replace after the bag was emptied. The whole con-traption was unstable and toppled over whenever you tried to tug it along behind you. Every second month or so, the monster broke down and was expensive to repair. Finally we gave up on the infuriating machine and I was able to obtain an American model from a departing diplomat. Even then I couldn't win; the Peking customs staff hit me hard for import duties when I had paper dust-bags sent in from the United States.

Since then I have come to realize that there probably is some method behind the apparent madness of making convenience appliances so hard to come by (though, heavens knows, there is a real need for items such as vacuum cleaners in Peking, where the strong winds from Mongolia drive so much dust into the home). China maintains nationwide austerity in its consumption of electric power—mostly generated from coal. The power is considered to be more important for production and lighting than for personal comfort. Hence, I assume, the state's deliberate policy of not marketing high-class household electric machines at reasonable prices.

In a commune workshop, two peasants weave baskets that will be used by restaurants to steam food. Communes often sell handicrafts in the city to raise cash.

A perfectly logical—and usually very simple—reason is almost always to be found for the way things are organized in Peking. To cite another example, food is bought in small quantities because almost no one possesses a refrigerator in which to store perishable foodstuffs (an additional reason is the great stress placed on freshness in Chinese cuisine).

Similarly, the prohibition on private buying and selling—except on a very trivial scale—explains the existence in Peking of a large number of so-called commission stores, which specialize in secondhand goods. If a family wishes to raise cash by disposing of some old clothes, an obsolete sewing-machine or whatever, the custom is to take the goods to a commission store, where they will be put on display and sold at a small profit to the state. In these stores one is likely to see all manner of junk: a wheezy, broken-down harmonium from a former mission school, a shaggy sheepskin coat, rusty ice-skates, old cameras, watches, electrical equipment, shoes and hats—in short, anything that might conceivably be put back to use. The people of Peking will readily buy damaged items, since the city has repair facilities for almost every item imaginable.

The main reason for foreigners to visit commission stores is to obtain furniture at a low price. I first entered a commission shop one windy November day when my wife and I were on Lo Mah Shih Ta Chieh (Camel and Horse Market Street), a couple of blocks from our temporary quarters in a hotel in the southern sector of Peking. An early winter dust-storm was sending a yellow swirl along the pavements. Outside the store, a group of people—muffled and damp-eyed with cold—were examining some old bedsteads. I didn't want to go inside (a feeling of diffidence always afflicts me when entering a building—be it a temple or a shop—that is utterly characteristic of someone else's culture). But Judy is a compulsive curiosity hunter, for whom the exploration of commission shops was to become an obsession, and she literally pulled me through the open doorway.

As invariably happens when a foreigner shows his face inside a Peking shop used mainly by Chinese, we were immediately surrounded by local shoppers curious to see the free side-show of an alien customer in action. Moreover—and this is especially irritating for the foreigner wishing to demonstrate his civilized manners and democratic nature—we were automatically given priority service. There is certainly an element of genuine courtesy in the Chinese practice of turning every foreign customer into a reluctant queue-jumper. But the principal purpose, I believe, is to eliminate, as expeditiously as possible, the distraction caused by the irregular shopper. Whatever the reasons, regular business seemed to be frozen for our benefit and the eyes of all other shoppers followed us around.

Amid a vast assortment of shoddy and well-worn goods, only one item attracted us: a pair of plain red-lacquered chairs, sadly in need of a good scrub-down and a fresh coat of lacquer, but temptingly priced at 35 yuan the pair. At the cash desk we received a flimsy green receipt with the words

Sumptuous silk robes that once graced the Peking stage line the walls of a Chung Wen Men street antique shop noted for its collection of theatrical costumes. The robes—regarded as relics of a decadent cultural past—are sold only to foreigners. The embroidered dragon's head at right decorates one of the garments on sale.

"English journalist" portentously inscribed in the top left-hand corner (Peking shopkeepers are supposed to record the identity of every foreign purchaser). Then, carrying the chairs before us in a posture suggestive of advanced pregnancy, we returned to our hotel. Our prizes were viewed with amused bewilderment by one of the attendants, who could not understand why any foreigner should want such junk.

Shortly afterwards, when we moved into a brand-new apartment and put the chairs under the shower, it seemed that half the dirt of Peking flowed muddily from their interstices. Somehow the original lacquer had acquired a picturesque patina of grime *under* the crackly finish; and so, on the advice of a friend, we applied an overcoat of shellac and red dye. It was a mistake. When mixed with alcohol, this shellac gives a soft and lustrous finish, less harsh than that of plain lacquer. Unfortunately, it is resoluble in human perspiration. Came the summer heat and our first luncheon guests had their shirts and trousers involuntarily smeared in red just before they had to attend an interview with an important Peking trading corporation. After that, in building up a collection of eight dining-room chairs, we reverted to clear lacquer to protect their exquisite finish.

How do the people of Peking react to seeing their secondhand shops overwhelmed by foreigners who are apparently endowed with more money than sense? On the whole they seem indifferent. They are mainly interested in more utilitarian and less old-fashioned things; it seems likely that they are not disposed to spend a significant slice of their earnings on objects of merely prestige or sentimental value.

The Chinese authorities, on the other hand, have shown considerable disquiet at the amount of their country's heritage that is being taken abroad. Until the mid-1970s the People's Republic had a ban on the export of anything made before 1800. Now that ban has been extended to any items more than 100 years old. Some objects, irrespective of age, may be restricted if they are judged to be of outstanding artistic quality; and no furniture made from China's rare rosewoods can be exported. This means that the overseas visitor to Peking is now denied the pleasure of acquiring anything truly antique unless, of course, he is content to keep it in China.

These export restrictions are perfectly understandable when one considers how the treasures of China's ancient culture have been plundered in the past. For example, in 1860, when Peking was occupied by French and British troops, the soldiers looted the old Summer Palace, then burned it to the ground. After the Boxer Rebellion in 1900, foreign soldiers gained entry to the Forbidden City and made off with jade and jewellery, as well as precious silks and furs; even the wives of missionaries and diplomats in the foreign community joined in the scavenging.

Further losses followed the founding of the Chinese Republic in 1912 and the leadership's decision to allow the boy-emperor P'u-yi to remain in the Forbidden City. The emperor still lived amid imperial splendour (although his household of 3,000 eunuchs was reduced by two-thirds) and he was given an annual subsidy of four million ounces of silver. Yet he soon resorted to selling palace furnishings to boost his personal wealth. More alarmingly, corrupt court eunuchs smuggled out large quantities of *objets d'art* and set up their own antique shops in Peking. In 1923, as a counter-measure, the emperor ordered all the imperial treasures to be catalogued, starting with those items stored in the Palace of Established Happiness. Conveniently for the eunuch pilferers, a fire swept through the palace and other buildings before the inventory could be taken. The estimated loss: at least 6,000 irreplaceable relics.

Today, the world's largest and most valuable collection of ancient Chinese art works is not to be found in mainland China. It resides instead in the National Palace Museum on the island of Taiwan (Formosa), where the Nationalists display more than 250,000 items, including bronzes dating back about 35 centuries. All these priceless artefacts were first moved from Peking to Shanghai and then Nanking in 1933, after the Japanese invasion of Manchuria. Later they were transferred to temples and caves in Kweichow and Szechwan provinces, where they remained hidden until the end of the Second World War. Finally, between 1947 and 1949, as the Communists advanced to power, the hoard was spirited away to Formosa.

Outsiders sometimes assume that the Communist leaders, so dedicated to forging a new society, have never really cared about their cultural heritage; but this is not the case. In December, 1948, for example, when Communist forces were on the verge of storming the gates of Peking, General Lin Piao abandoned his most favoured point of attack simply because an architect advised him that it would destroy a rare section of unrestored Ming architecture. And since then, largely through exhaustive archaeological excavations, the Communists have done much in building up new collections of Chinese antiquities.

The Peking Palace Museum boasts an incredible trove: spectacular sculptures and carvings, cloisonné, tapestry, embroidery, millennia-old bronzes and rare books that were printed with engraved blocks centuries before printing was known in Europe. These items are displayed to evince the skill and patience of the Chinese craftsman and, more pointedly, the unrelenting selfishness of a ruling class that spent immense fortunes on such extravagances at a time when millions of their subjects were often starving. The official Party policy does not encourage art for art's sake. Like everything else, art must have socio-political relevance.

Peking is no longer a paradise for the fine arts collector. At the same time, just as the workings of present-day China can be glimpsed in department stores or even commission stores, the richness of the past is generously evoked by Peking's many small art shops. There you will find an enormous range of interesting *objets d'art*, curios and souvenirs: superb modern

A veteran employee of the Arts and Crafts Factory, using the cloisonné technique to decorate a plate, carefully applies wet enamel to a pattern of raised wire.

Old Crafts Renewed

During the centuries of imperial rule, Peking enjoyed a glittering reputation as a centre of the applied arts. After the loss of court patronage following the republican revolution of 1911, that reputation went into eclipse. But it has recently been revived in the workshops of a state-run enterprise called the Arts and Crafts Factory, which caters largely to the export trade. The factory employs more than a thousand craftsmen to produce jade and ivory carvings, paintings, cloisonné and lacquerware. Apprentices earn about 20 yuan ($11) a month, but a few highly skilled workers make 10 times as much, putting them close to the compensation level of a senior physician.

One of the factory's master craftsmen adds paint to the rim of a snuff bottle.

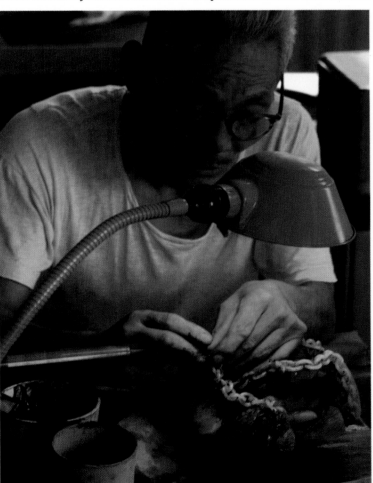

A worker polishes a jade chain with abrasive paste and a grinding wheel.

A bespectacled apprentice—one of roughly 450 women on the Peking Arts and Crafts Factory's payroll—uses an electric drill to sculpt an ivory figurine.

Famous buildings, among them the Eiffel Tower and the Leaning Tower of Pisa, adorn a sculpture carved by a Peking artist from a single elephant tusk.

copies of old porcelain pieces and bronzes, fine reproductions of traditional painting, jade and ivory sculptures, brassware, enamels, lacquerware, lace and embroidery, jewellery, snuff containers, scrolls, calligraphies, rubbings and all manner of novelties, such as cages for singing crickets, pigeon whistles and *nei-hua* (miniature bottles with pictures painted on the inside).

My own speciality as an amateur collector was mandarins' hat-buttons—spherical or oval badges of rank, usually about an inch high and mounted on a worked bronze base. Mandarins of the last imperial dynasty, the Ch'ing (1644-1912), introduced such buttons to proclaim their position: a ruby badge for a provincial governor, with lesser ranks symbolized by coral, sapphire, lapis lazuli, white jade, gold or silver. By the 19th Century the mandarinate was too impoverished to buy most of the materials that were supposed to be used in hat-buttons, and so almost all the buttons now to be found in Peking are made of such substitutes as coloured glass (a Peking speciality) or the shells of giant clams. But, because of their high rank, ruby and coral hat-buttons, to my knowledge, were never debased. I managed to obtain two coral buttons in Liu Li Ch'ang, a *hu-t'ung* located a few blocks south-west of Ch'ien Men.

Liu Li Ch'ang takes its name from the Glazed Tile Works established there in the 15th Century to produce colourful glazed tiles for the new Ming palaces and pavilions. In the late 18th Century it developed into a great market for curios, antiques, paintings, old books and scrolls; and subsequently it became famous for its Chinese New Year Fair. The fair is no longer held and the number of shops has drastically declined, especially since the 1966 Cultural Revolution, when Liu Li Ch'ang was coldly renamed Anti-Feudalism Street. Nevertheless, it remains Peking's most interesting centre for truly traditional art shops.

In this *hu-t'ung* I often frequented a delightful shop run by two shy old men who sold prints of famous stone carvings and replicas of T'ang ceramic figures. In the West, the word "replica" suggests some cheap, mass-produced imitation, but in Peking it can sometimes mean a modern copy that may look even better, both artistically and technically, than the centuries-old original (*pace* the connoisseurs). It was certainly true of replicas in this shop. They sold me a superb replica of a Han dynasty tomb figure: a four-foot high, hollow clay horse with a removable head and tail, and moulded, so it was claimed, of clay from the exact source used for the originals some 2,000 years ago.

Prices are not low. In Liu Li Ch'ang, I went into a scroll and fan-painting shop where they coolly unrolled a simple painting of a flower by the great 20th-Century artist Ch'i Pai-shih and invited me to invest 17,000 yuan ($9,000) in it. They know the market value of their treasures, but they are not unreasonably profit-minded.

I soon concluded, however, that scroll-hunting in Peking is a tedious and embarrassing business, one strictly for a thick-skinned customer. It takes a measure of sang-froid to stand by while shop attendants untie the ribbon around each sample and carefully unroll it for your inspection—a procedure requiring at least two pairs of hands. After humming and hawing over a dozen or more scrolls, many people feel morally obliged to buy at least one. In fact, there is no reason why you should not pass an innocent hour in this fashion; the assistants have nothing else to do, and they do not stand to gain or lose a commission on the sale. And if you still feel obligated, you can always opt for a comparatively cheap fan-painting or a small block of doodlings by some minor literatus of the late Ch'ing or early Republican period.

Our own solution, eventually, was not to look for scrolls in Peking, but to go out and get them made. In the western sector of Liu Li Ch'ang, there was a shop specializing in the austere tools of the painter's and calligrapher's art: ink-boxes, ink-stones, brush-stands, inscribed paper-weights, and an adjustable rhombic device that enables the calligrapher to keep his brushwork in a straight vertical line. The shop also sold prints and old rubbings of stone carvings; and conveniently, just across the street, was a small workshop where two old men and a girl practised the highly skilled craft of mounting flimsy paper works of art on thick, silk-faced scroll paper, then adding at one end the wooden roller that enables the scroll either to be displayed or neatly stored.

The workshop was a cheery place. A big kettle sang permanently on a glowing, cast-iron stove in winter, and one wall was decorated by a charming painting of some elderly Chinese gentlemen squatting in a pavilion beside a waterfall. I could never persuade them to sell the painting; but the staff were particularly friendly and it was fascinating to watch the girl plying a big hair-brush dipped in some farinaceous paste and precisely lining up the fragile sheets of often-damaged art work that had to be mounted. Then, sadly and suddenly, everything changed.

I made the mistake of trying to photograph the craftsmen at work. Only my timing was at fault. My visit to the workshop happened to coincide with one of those periodic spasms of political activity in Peking when people didn't relish the prospect of being asked by their local cadre to explain how their picture came to be splashed on the pages of some "bourgeois" foreign news magazine. They positively resented the intrusion and so I never went there again.

Early in our stay, Judy and I enjoyed visiting a high-class junk shop in Liu Li Ch'ang that was run by a fat and jolly old man. I suspected that he was the original owner of the shop and—as happened to many proprietors after nationalization in 1949—had been allowed to remain in charge as a "government manager". Now, somewhat late in life, he was trying to learn English—a study that became all the rage in Peking in the early 1970s. He always kept a dog-eared Chinese/English dictionary close at hand; and whenever we entered the shop, he would greet us with enthusiasm and then immediately bombard us with questions about how certain words should be pronounced. We called him Mr. Ginger, because his name—Chiang—meant just that.

In 1974, however, Mr. Ginger disappeared from the curio shop. His place was taken by a group of rather surly and unknowledgeable young women who became even more surly when foreigners commented on the unconscionable rise in prices that had accompanied the change of management. For a serious collector, the shop became a very poor place indeed, selling mostly third-rate stone Buddhas (labelled "human figures" to avoid religious reference), over-priced lacquer boxes and snuff containers, and Ch'ing courtesans' enamel hairpins.

In so many ways, I am assailed by regrets in reviewing the more orderly and organized shopping scene that now prevails in Peking. I regret that the sale of antiques and curios to foreigners has been taken over more and more by the big Friendship Store—an ill-named and soulless cavern that opened near the main diplomatic quarter in 1973. I regret that department stores in general are now increasingly fulfilling the function of small street shops where one could come to know the proprietor and find extra dimensions in a transaction. I regret the ghastly movement towards political orthodoxy in art, as represented by the Jung Pao Chai, a once-distinguished emporium on Liu Li Ch'ang, which now specializes in heroic scrolls of workers, peasants and soldiers, and New Year's greeting cards depicting modernized duck-farms and forests of pylons.

But all this is to criticize minutiae in the picture of material progress that is modern Peking. One has to recognize that, for most Chinese, the plusses outweigh the minuses. Exploring Liu Li Ch'ang may not be the exciting adventure it once was; but then, except for visitors, shopping in Peking is not intended to be entertainment. Rather, it is an object lesson in a new kind of living—conclusive evidence that this city has managed to eliminate the most grinding poverty and provide an adequate supply of food and essential goods for its millions.

Shopping in a Planned Economy

Workers gather outside a store offering products of China's burgeoning electronics industry. Window-shopping and browsing are habitual pastimes in Peking.

In a city full of reminders of the ideals and priorities of the state, perhaps the most insistent reminder of all is the shopping scene—which the state regulates down to the smallest details of prices and inventory. Nearly all the goods for sale are Chinese-made, and 80 per cent of them are produced in Peking itself. Because little attempt is made to entice buyers by means of attractive packaging or display, the stores have something of the austere atmosphere of supply depots. But the service is normally efficient and courteous, in part because the counter assistants—who ring up sales on abacuses instead of cash registers—are trained to be helpful to their customers at daily self-criticism sessions. As for business hours, the state sees to it that customer-convenience is at a maximum: most shops and stores stay open from 9 a.m. to 7 p.m. seven days a week.

A display of plaster figurines, popular as home decorations, attracts a crowd in the Hundred Goods Emporium.

Markets for the Masses

The proudest monuments to state-controlled consumerism in Peking are the dozen or so department stores—multi-storey edifices that bear resounding names like the Hundred Goods Emporium and stock virtually all the wares a family needs. But an earlier shopping style can still be seen in a few surviving bazaars, each jammed with scores of speciality stalls. Most everyday shopping is done at neighbourhood stores and open-air food markets.

An array of household goods that includes feather dusters, brushes and round-bottomed frying-pans—called woks—fills the shelves of a Tung Tan street store.

Customers at the Hundred Goods Emporium's sports counter can choose from a lavish variety of table-tennis bats, or take home a made-in-Peking shuttlecock.

Tiers of fine-tipped brushes for writing and painting fill a display-case.

Calligraphers can find all they need for their art in this shop on Liu Li Ch'ang street. To inspire them, a framed poem in Mao's own hand hangs from the ceiling.

A jet airliner behind the toy counter at the Hundred Goods Emporium draws ranks of admirers, but with a price tag of $5 it may wait some time for a buyer.

6

Preserving the Revolution

On May 25, 1966, Miss Nieh Yüan-tzu, a philosophy lecturer at Peking University, put up a wall poster signed by herself and six colleagues. The poster denounced Lu Ping, president of the university and first secretary of its Party committee, for not giving sufficient emphasis to Maoist doctrines, and it urged "all revolutionary intellectuals" to "go into battle holding high the great red banner of Mao Tse-tung's thought". Unaccustomed to such an audacious challenge, the Party committee—which was controlled by elements hostile to Mao's radicalism—struck back swiftly and savagely, condemning the dissidents as "traitors" and "careerists".

At first, it seemed that the counter-attack would be successful. But Miss Nieh and her friends had a powerful behind-the-scenes patron—Mao Tse-tung himself. Mao had been convinced for some time that China was in need of intensive ideological purification and he made sure the poster was given nation-wide publicity. As a result, the rebellion at Peking University took hold, and within weeks millions of young people across the land were joining in a massive and unprecedented campaign against established authority. As Mao later implied, "the poster of the seven" was really the opening shot of the Great Proletarian Cultural Revolution, a crisis for Peking and all of China.

Although this bizarre upheaval came to an end in 1968, it was symptomatic of a problem that Mao had still not resolved by the time of his death in 1976: How was China to ensure its future as a great industrial power without creating a privileged intelligentsia and thus compromising the ultimate objective of a classless society? No other single issue has been so divisive or has contributed in quite the same measure to Peking's isolation from the rest of the world. The question bothered Mao for most of his political life, a fact that is almost certainly related to his own experiences as a young man at Peking University.

Founded in 1898 by the Society for the Strengthening of Learning, a movement that aimed to modernize China through the introduction of Western knowledge, Peking University had been viewed mainly as a stepping stone to an easy and lucrative career. Professors and students alike had gained a low reputation for loose morals—or so it is related today—and the university is said to have been known by epithets such as "The Brothel Brigade" and "The Gambling Den".

By 1918, however, when Mao arrived from the southern province of Hunan to take on the job of assistant librarian, the university had acquired a new image. Professor Ts'ai Yuan-p'ei, who served as Minister of Education

Undergraduates pore over textbooks in a library at Ch'ing-hua University, Peking's foremost engineering institute. Campus life is strictly regimented and academic work is only one part of it: time must also be found for political activity and—as one student-athlete's numbered sports shirt suggests—for organized exercise.

A key aim of the curricula in Peking schools is
to link theoretical knowledge with practical
application. Here, a young student experiments
on the arm of a classmate to learn the basics of
acupuncture—the ancient art of healing by
inserting needles strategically into the body.

in the cabinet of Sun Yat-sen, China's first great revolutionary leader, was
now Chancellor; and under his influence the university had become a
hotbed of radical ideas. Ch'en Tu-hsiu, who later became the first General
Secretary of the Chinese Communist Party, was made dean of the school
of literature; and he was soon joined by Hu Shih, a leader of the campaign
for a vernacular style of literature that would make it possible to propagate
progressive ideas in language that would be intelligible to the common
people. To the newly arrived young man from Hunan, however, the
brightest star in this radical firmament was Li Ta-chao, the university's chief
librarian and China's leading Marxist philosopher. Mao had trained as a
teacher in Hunan, and it was one of his old instructors who got Li Ta-chao
to offer Mao the job of assistant librarian.

In his own vivid account of those formative months, Mao has written of
the contrast between his "miserable" living conditions and the beauty of
the Imperial City, in which the university was then located. "I stayed in a
little room which held seven other people. When we were all packed fast
on the *k'ang* (a stone bed heated from underneath by a fire) there was
scarcely room enough for any of us to breathe. I used to have to warn
people on each side of me when I wanted to turn over. But in the parks
and the old palace grounds I saw the early northern spring. I saw the white
plum blossom flower while the ice still held solid over Pei Hai Park. I saw
the willows over the lake with the ice crystals hanging from them."

No less striking for Mao was the contrast between the professed beliefs
and the personal behaviour of many university firebrands. Checking out
books or writing down the names of those who came to read newspapers
and magazines, he was treated to the daily discussions of "bourgeois
radicals" who deplored the wretched plight of the Chinese people, yet
"had no time to listen to an assistant librarian speaking a southern dialect".

In a workshop attached to Peking Middle School No. 31, a schoolgirl operates a metal-punching machine as part of the state's education programme. Pupils may spend one afternoon a week, performing tasks that range from making light bulbs to producing spare parts for cars.

Once Mao tried to talk to the celebrated Dr. Hu Shih, but the latter flatly ignored him. As Mao explains, "My office was so low that people avoided me; to most of them I did not exist as a human being."

Although the university undoubtedly had its fair share of those whom Mao contemptuously dismissed as "talking machines", it did succeed in generating a great deal more than hot air. In 1917, China had entered the First World War on the side of the Allies, and most Chinese confidently expected the Paris Peace Conference to rescind the humiliating 19th-Century treaties that had divided their country into foreign "spheres of influence". But on May 3, 1919, the students at Peking University learned that German semi-colonial rights in Shantung were to be transferred to Japan. The next day, students took to the streets demanding the restoration of Chinese sovereignty in the province and their protest quickly snowballed into a nation-wide anti-imperialist movement that included merchants, industrialists and workers.

The May Fourth Movement, as it came to be known, had been sparked by foreign oppression, but much of its anger was directed at targets closer to home. For 2,500 years Chinese life had been cast in the rigidly conservative mould of Confucianism, and it was this tyranny of tradition that came to be singled out as the root cause of China's chronic failure to cope with the modern world. So vigorous and widespread was the upsurge against the old system of values and ideas that some modern historians refer to it as China's First Cultural Revolution. Mao himself, who had gone back to Hunan to work as a primary school teacher only a few weeks before the spark was struck in Peking, certainly regarded the explosive events of 1919 in that sense; and when he returned to the city 30 years later as the head of a Communist government, he was determined that the nation should experience a second and much more profound transformation.

One of the new government's first priorities was to purge the educational system of Western influence. This was particularly evident at Yen-ching and Ch'ing-hua universities, which were located in the north-west suburbs of Peking. The United States had provided money for their foundation from the indemnity that China was forced to pay after the siege of the foreign legations in the Boxer uprising of 1900; and both institutions had more affinity with the Ivy League than with either Confucianism or Communism. At Yen-ching (meaning Swallow Capital, the literary name for the city of Peking) students were always addressed with the prefix Mister or Miss, and even classes on the Chinese language were conducted, as far as it was possible, in English.

To the Communists, this situation epitomized the imperialist domination of China. In 1950 Ch'ing-hua University was reorganized as China's leading engineering institute. Neighbouring Yen-ching first was closed down: then in 1953 its spacious campus, originally designed as the pleasure ground of an 18th-Century Manchu courtier, became the new site of Peking University. To underline the break with the past, the university was redesignated Pei-ta, the Chinese abbreviation of its name, Pei-ching ta-hsüeh. More than a dozen other prestigious educational institutes, including the Chinese Academy of Sciences, were also moved out to the north-west suburbs, turning the area into the academic heartland of the Chinese People's Republic.

This did, not, however, mean the end of foreign domination of the Chinese educational system. Faced with 90 per cent illiteracy and a desperate shortage of teachers, China's new government had little option but to rely upon extensive aid from the U.S.S.R. The result was an almost slavish acceptance of Soviet teaching methods and standards. Russian was adopted as the major foreign language; and even curricula, textbooks and teaching materials in Chinese were simply literal translations from the Russian, with no allowance made for local needs and conditions.

The hangover from this period can be seen still in the second-hand book section of the East Wind Department Store on Wang Fu Ching street. About half the items for sale are out-of-date Russian manuals on science and engineering; and there is usually a small group of middle-aged people flipping through them—people who learned Russian in the 1950s and whose knowledge continues to be useful because much modern Chinese technology is still based on early Soviet designs. In fact, Russian remained the number-one foreign language taught in Chinese colleges and universities until 1972, when it began to be overtaken by English.

China's pressing need for skilled technicians and administrators also meant that scarce university places were awarded mainly to those who had already benefited from middle schooling. Such people naturally tended to come from the formerly well-to-do classes—landlords, rich peasants, industrialists, intellectuals—so that the situation was not much different

On the pavement outside a technical institute in north-west Peking, teachers help peasants husk grain that has been brought by truck from a neighbouring commune. Many of the colleges that are concentrated on this semi-rural edge of the city have agreements with communes to provide assistance during sowing or harvesting.

from the one that had existed prior to 1949. And just as the old Imperial education system had been geared to creating a privileged and almost priestly caste of Confucian scholars, so the new Sovietized system was geared to creating an equally lofty and no less privileged caste of experts and intellectuals. There were highly differentiated pay scales for graduates and non-graduates; and scientists and professors enjoyed salaries many times those of workers and peasants.

The gradual introduction of compulsory schooling in all but the most inaccessible parts of China led to an increase in the number of working- and peasant-class youngsters qualifying for university training, and by 1955 the proportion of such students at Pei-ta alone had been raised to 28 per cent. Although this was no small achievement, it hardly provided a basis for the radically new social order that Mao envisaged. In 1957, therefore, he launched his first major "rectification" campaign; and in 1958 the Party laid down the principle that "Education must serve politics, must be combined with productive labour, and must be led by the Party". Stressing the importance of this new principle, Mao pointedly declared that "to import Soviet codes and conventions inflexibly is to lack the creative spirit".

The aim was not only to make students and teachers more "proletarian" in outlook, but also to mobilize the whole of the nation's resources for the Great Leap Forward—the ambitious programme of rapid industrial expansion that began in 1958. Everyone was urged to secure socialism "by going all out to build more, faster, better, and more economically", and whole weeks of the academic calendar were taken up with work in factories or on the newly organized agricultural collectives known as "people's communes". Schools and universities themselves became "centres of production", growing their own food and running their own blast furnaces and workshops. According to one report, Ch'ing-hua University set up no fewer than 60 plants, shops and factories between 1958 and 1961. It is also said to have completed more than 900 major projects in scientific research and in trial manufacture of new products, including a model 2,000-kilowatt electric power station.

All too often, however, quality was sacrificed for quantity. In the frantic effort to achieve ever increasing output, precision machines were ruined by over-use and much of the steel turned out by the backyard blast furnaces fell far short of industrial requirements. Forced to devote an increasing amount of their time to productive labour, students had little opportunity to master their subjects. It was later revealed, for example, that a lecturer at Ch'ing-hua allowed only 90 minutes to explain six geometrical curves, with 15 minutes for each curve (he timed himself with a watch).

Three successive years of calamitous weather conditions and the withdrawal, in 1960, of all assistance by an increasingly hostile Soviet Union brought the Great Leap Forward to a grinding halt in 1961. Economic recovery now took precedence over political dogma; and the obvious need for properly trained personnel to fill the gap left by Soviet technicians meant that study once more became the main concern of such places as Ch'ing-hua and Pei-ta. Students accepted the reversal with an enthusiasm that astonished the authorities. According to an observer in 1962, "There are no vacant chairs to be found in libraries, either by day or in the evening. In some schools the students line up waiting for a seat. Everybody wants to study. . . . With the concession of this new freedom, freedom to study, the students have dashed to their books with the same eagerness as students elsewhere dash to illicit pleasures, or to the playing fields."

It was reported that, in addition to the one foreign language they were required to study, students at Ch'ing-hua were trying to learn a second or even a third; and the authorities warned against the dangers of trying to learn too much too quickly. A cause of much greater concern to Mao was the reappearance of what he regarded as the old educational élitism. The number of university students from worker and peasant families was being drastically reduced because of the renewed emphasis on proven academic ability. Many schools in Peking and other major cities virtually became private academies for the children of influential officials.

David Milton, an American who taught English in Peking from 1964 to 1969, has described the situation at the Peking University middle school, where two of his sons enrolled in 1965. "The physical layout was similar to that of many older high schools in the United States. The instruction, following the Russian model, was more formal; students were required to stand up whenever the teacher entered the room, teaching consisted of formal lecturing with little discussion by students, and homework and examinations were rigorous. Many of the students were the sons of army officers, government officials and intellectuals; they were all college bound."

On a commune near a Peking machine-tool factory, two farmers follow horsedrawn ploughs. Most communes cultivate land by traditional methods.

Mao tried to counter the élitist trend with a Socialist Education Movement that stressed the continuing danger posed by "reactionary classes". As time went on, however, he became convinced that nothing short of an upheaval similar in scale to that of 1919 could prevent China from degenerating into a "revisionist" replica of the Soviet Union. Following the failure of the Great Leap Forward, a significant section of the Party leadership, including Liu Shao-ch'i, the head of state, had come to favour a much less doctrinaire approach to the country's economic development, and it was these heretical "enemies without guns" whom Mao planned to sweep away in the surging tide of a new Cultural Revolution.

But if the Party itself was infected with "revisionist" rot, who was to administer the antidote? In choosing the nation's youth for this crucial task, Mao intended not only to purge "those in authority in the Party who have taken the capitalist road", but also to provide the generation that had grown up since 1949 with revolutionary combat experience. As he told the French writer, André Malraux, in an interview in July, 1965: "The young are not born 'red', they have not known the revolution. . . . There is a whole generation of dogmatic youths, and dogma is less useful than cow dung. One can make whatever one likes out of it, even revisionism."

The "revisionist" stronghold was Peking, where the Party Committee led by P'eng Chen, who was also the Mayor, had encouraged a stream of barely disguised Press attacks on Mao and his radical policies. The most barbed of the published indictments was by Wu Han, the Deputy Mayor, who implied that Mao was behaving like a tyrannical Chinese emperor. Prevented by the Peking Party bureaucracy from publishing a counterblast in the newspapers of his own capital, Mao commissioned one of his supporters to denounce Wu Han through the *Shanghai Evening News*.

The attack was published in November, 1965, but it was not until five months later that Mao found an opportunity to launch a full-scale assault. On March 26, 1966, Liu Shao-ch'i left Peking on a diplomatic trip to Pakistan, Afghanistan and Burma; in his absence Maoist supporters seized control of the important Peking propaganda machine. P'eng Chen apparently was arrested the following week and, on April 19, the official Party newspaper, the *People's Daily*, warned of the impending deluge: "The great revolutionary waves will wash away all the filth of the bourgeois trends in art and literature. . . . Something must be destroyed and something must be set up in the course of the Socialist Cultural Revolution. Without destruction there can be no construction."

The deluge began with Miss Nieh Yüan-tzu's denunciatory wall poster of May 25 and, as the Chairman had anticipated, it engulfed and destroyed every suspected Maoist apostate, from the head of state downwards. After years of rigid discipline, it was heady stuff suddenly to be told by the "Great Helmsman" himself that "rebellion is justified!", and whatever feelings of intellectual superiority students may have been nursing gave way to the thrill of embarking on a great crusade. Formal classes were suspended as millions of young people, following the example of the Peking students, mobilized themselves into Red Guard units and swept through the country waving their little red books of Mao quotations and dragging out "freaks and monsters" for public pillorying. In the words of the Red Guards of Ch'ing-hua University middle school: "We [will] turn the old world upside down, smash it to pieces, pulverize it, create chaos and make a tremendous mess, the bigger the better! Make rebellion in a big way, rebel to the end! We are bent on creating a tremendous proletarian uproar, and hewing out a proletarian new world!"

Much of what went on during the Cultural Revolution was farcical or grotesque. Many of Peking's streets were given new names with a suitably revolutionary flavour: Wang Fu Ching, one of the city's main thorough-fares, was changed, for example, to "People's Road", and Chiao Min Hsiang, the street that had once housed foreign embassies, and was said to have been barred to "dogs and Chinese", was renamed "Anti-Imperialist Street". One Red Guard unit even suggested to Premier Chou En-lai that the city's traffic-light regulations should be changed so that red would mean "go". (Chou tactfully rejected the proposal.) Another incident —possibly apocryphal—involved the Foreign Minister, Ch'en Yi, whom the Red Guards had forced to sit on a platform wearing a dunce's cap. The story has it that Ch'en Yi suddenly looked at his watch and said, "Please excuse me, I have to go to the airport to welcome the President of Guinea." What his young detractors replied is not on record.

Other manifestations of Red Guard fervour were rather less humorous. Veteran Party members resented the strident lectures of adolescents, and in some parts of the country, peasants and workers physically resisted the incursion of young Maoist fanatics. In their determination to root out "revisionists", the witch-hunters began denouncing one another, and several university campuses, including that of Ch'ing-hua, were turned into battlefields by rival factions of Red Guards. Mao had written many years before that a revolution was "not the same thing as inviting people to dinner, or painting a picture, or doing fancy needlework", but even he was alarmed by the eruption of paranoia and violence.

"I did something disastrously wrong," he confessed to a meeting of Communist Party officials held in October, 1966. "I approved Nieh Yüan-tzu's poster and wrote a letter to the Ch'ing-hua University middle school, as well as writing a poster of my own entitled 'Bombard the Head-quarters'. I myself had not forseen that as soon as the Peking University poster was broadcast, the whole country would be thrown into turmoil. Red Guards had mobilized throughout the country, and in one rush they swept you off your feet. Since it was I who caused the havoc, it is under-standable if you have some bitter words for me."

In an iron-and-steel mill that employs 30,000 people, two workers attach a hook to a giant ladle before tipping its contents of molten scrap metal into a furnace. Assisted by abundant local coal and iron-ore deposits, Peking—which was almost completely lacking in industry before 1949—has become the fifth-ranking industrial city in China.

Mao called for an end to "extreme anarchism". But it was not until the autumn of 1967, when teams of army mediators were sent into the schools, universities and factories, that some semblance of public order was restored; and it was to be a further 12 months before the violence was finally halted. At Ch'ing-hua, for example, two rival Red Guard factions ignored appeals from the army and, in April, 1968, their preliminary skirmishing turned into a desperate and bloody battle in which both sides used bombs, grenades, rockets, rifles and machine-guns.

The battle went on until July, when some 30,000 workers from Peking were mobilized by the authorities and marched on to the campus, calling upon the students to cease firing. One faction, however, regarded this latest mediation attempt as a "revisionist" trick and, after fighting its way through the ranks of unarmed workers, fled into the countryside, hoping to link up with "true Mao Tse-tung supporters". By the end of the day, more than 700 people had been injured and five lay dead.

"You have let me down," Mao is reported to have told the feuding Red Guard leaders later that summer, "and what is more, you have disappointed the workers, peasants and army men of China." He made it clear that in future they were to be subject to army and "proletarian" political discipline. In December he got the troublemakers out of Peking and other cities by directing all "educated young people to go to the countryside to be re-educated by the poor and lower-middle peasants".

With the Red Guards firmly under control, Mao was able to launch the second and perhaps most important phase of the Cultural Revolution: the radical reorganization of higher education. Instead of entering a university directly from school, young people had first to spend at least two years working on a commune, in a factory, or doing military service. The various work units would nominate candidates mainly on the basis, not of their academic ability, but of their "proletarian" attitude, or "redness". Given sufficient "redness", it was held that training would naturally lead to "expertness" in any line of endeavour, but without sufficient "redness", "expertness" was held to be impossible, however much training was given. As Mao told his nephew, Mao Yüan-hsin: "Class struggle is your most important subject, and it is compulsory."

Although the present Chinese leadership has switched the emphasis from "redness" to "expertness", Mao's injunction to combine work and study still holds. As at the time of the Great Leap Forward, schools and universities operate their own factories and workshops, and teachers and students are required to devote a minimum of four weeks a year to outside farming or factory work. Pei-ta, in addition to running seven big workshops of its own, has links with 60 enterprises outside the university, including the Peking People's Machine Tool Factory and a commune. "We want workers to be intellectuals and intellectuals to be workers," Pei-ta's director of revolutionary education explained to a group of foreign visitors. "Why should students be locked up in school and kept apart from workers, peasants and soldiers? What we really want to do is run our schools with the doors open. We want our schools to be in society, not above it."

Adapting education to the needs of society as a whole is an ideal shared by many in the West, but for the Chinese it has particular relevance and urgency. Before Mao launched the Cultural Revolution, the country's intellectuals rarely took any serious account of practical considerations. After Mao insisted on marrying theory with practice, some scientists bothered looking into the problem of agricultural development at first hand, while some peasants troubled to study methodology and then came up with ideas for new seed strains.

Judged in purely Western terms, however, the Maoist educational experiment can hardly be counted a great success. The emphasis on political rectitude rather than academic achievement discouraged the maximum use of human talent; and the disapproval of any theoretical research unrelated to short-term practical problems retarded the country's scientific and industrial development. I once gravely offended the officials of a machine-tool plant by questioning their insistence on the importance of practical work—on the grounds that some of the greatest practical developments of the 20th Century were based on the theoretical discoveries of Einstein. They seemed not to have heard of Einstein or the Theory of Relativity, although that may have been just a problem of translation.

Educational standards declined to such an extent that the armed forces and many big industrial concerns felt obliged to set up specialized training and research institutes for the brightest of their own people. It was the work done in these places that enabled China to make headway with her nuclear and space-satellite programmes—something that would have been impossible if the country had been relying entirely on universities like Ch'ing-hua and Pei-ta. As Chairman Hua Kuo-feng's regime made clear in 1977, the "harassment and persecution" of intellectuals had seriously undermined China's chances of achieving superpower status by the end of the century.

Obsessed with his dislike for the scholar and the expert, Mao was unconcerned by the fact that both were necessary for increased production and rising living standards. As he saw it, doing a good job of production "in no way refers to increased output. Rather it depends on whether or not we have aroused the revolutionary activity of the masses."

Having suppressed one form of élitism, however, Mao succeeded only in replacing it with another. "Redness" became the new passport to professional status; and by parroting Marxist and Maoist texts, people were able to gain positions well above the level merited by their academic or technical qualifications. It was really just a variation on the age-old theme: the Confucian mandarin sat in his prefecture oblivious to the social

Coping with Calamity

"Unite and struggle; man will overcome nature." So stated a brave slogan that appeared all over Peking after an earth tremor—an all-too-familiar event in the region—damaged 30,000 buildings during the summer of 1976. Because further major quakes were expected, the entire population was instructed to move into the open.

At first, people simply carried their beds outside; later, huts were devised of everything from scraps of wood to mud and matted straw. With the onset of winter, most of the populace moved indoors again; but, by official decree, the makeshift shelters were left standing as insurance against any future earthquakes occurring. Peking, after all, had been lucky: in the city of Tangshan, only 90 miles away to the southeast, the collapse of buildings during the quake had cost more than half a million lives.

Obeying radio exhortations, a family camps outside their home amid a jumble of furniture.

Carrying on their usual trade in the open air, "temporary barbers"—as a sign on the front of these premises calls them—work through a line-up of patrons.

Roadside sewer pipes provide ready-made shelter for some residents of north Peking. The brick-weighted strings are used to secure coverings at the pipe ends.

A semi-permanent cabin of wattle and mud offers privacy and a modicum of comfort during earthquake alerts. Left-over building straw hangs above the window.

needs of his district; the "radical" professor sat in his university oblivious to the educational needs of his students.

As was widely admitted in the Chinese Press in 1974, there was also a re-emergence of the old caste system. Senior Party officials and high-ranking army officers were successfully pulling strings to get their children admitted to university after they had been—according to the local vernacular—"gold-plated" by a two-year stint on a commune. This tactic must have been particularly galling to the millions of non-privileged youngsters who had also been transplanted from the relative comfort of urban areas, such as Peking, to the rural communes, but had very little hope of leaving even at the end of their two years.

Of all Mao's policies, that of "going down to the countryside" is the one that continues to cause most anguish. Because of the romantic propaganda surrounding it, many school-leavers set off with high hopes, or, as the Peking Press prefers to put it, with "red hearts". All too often, however, disillusion and despair set in among urban youths who are unprepared for the tough rural life. The tightly-knit communities to which they are sent tend to be resentful of the "well-educated" strangers; and youngsters from the big cities are not averse to showing their contempt for the "primitive" peasants. A significant number manage to slip back into the cities to lead a precarious existence without ration cards. If their families refuse to help them, they are forced to eke out a miserable living, perhaps as illegal street traders or cinema ticket touts, buying rice and clothing coupons on the black market.

For the few who are lucky enough to gain admission to a university, the future is suddenly full of promise. And if the university happens to be Pei-ta, it is likely to be full of political excitement, too. Ever since "the poster of the seven" went up in May, 1966, Pei-ta has been at once the laboratory and the barometer of Chinese political life. Floating ideas among student trusties was Mao's way of tackling opponents, real or imagined; every major political campaign since the Cultural Revolution has been launched through the posters of Pei-ta. The purpose of wall posters was described by the *People's Daily* soon after Miss Nieh Yüan-tzu and her friends had sparked off that first great conflagration: "Revolutionary posters are a mirror reflecting all freaks and monsters. They constitute the most effective means of mobilizing the masses freely to launch the most powerful attack on the enemy. All anti-Party and anti-socialist counter-revolutionary elements are most afraid of posters."

Once a campaign gets under way, lorry loads of workers from Peking and beyond are brought on to the campus to copy the posters for eventual reproduction in their offices, factories and communes. At such times, the Long March Restaurant, just across the road from the university, is crowded with workers from the provinces; and it is common to meet people who have come from as far away as the city of Tsientsin, about

Hand-tinted portraits which are intended as mementoes for friends and relatives smile from a photographer's studio on Wang Fu Ching street in central Peking. Above the framed prints, characters spelling out the slogan "Serve the People" make a tinsel contribution to the city's pervasive mood of social responsibility.

70 miles away. Towards the end of a campaign, one will also see masses of children copying down the sacred texts of Pei-ta with great seriousness.

The overwhelming majority of Pei-ta's 10,000 students are members either of the Communist Party or the Communist Youth League. (Party membership is permitted from the age of 18, and League membership from 14.) Joining commits them to at least one political meeting a week, although, in practice, they attend many more. There are meetings of the students' union, meetings of the department, meetings of the class—and just meetings. It is a never-ending process because every Chinese political campaign interlocks with the one before it.

When the former Defence Minister and Mao's "closest comrade-in-arms", Lin Piao, died in 1971, after allegedly attempting a coup against Mao, the nation-wide campaign to discredit him began gradually under the slogan "Criticize Revisionism and Rectify the Style of Work". Through the students and key officials, it soon became clear to most people that this was an attack on Lin Piao's hitherto shining reputation; and in 1973 the slogan was changed to "Criticize Lin Piao and Rectify the Style of Work". Six months later, this wording was superceded by "Criticize Lin Piao and Confucius". The philosopher had revered a nobleman named Chou, and so the real target of the campaign was taken to be the ailing premier, Chou En-lai, who was considered too moderate by the ultra-Leftists grouped around Mao's wife, Chiang Ch'ing.

Chou managed to keep ahead in this Byzantine power struggle, so the radicals switched their attention to the Deputy Premier, Teng Hsiao-p'ing, whom Chou was apparently grooming as his successor. Towards the end of 1975 special buses were actually provided to take foreign diplomats and journalists—myself included—to the fenced-off poster areas of Ch'ing-hua and Pei-ta. For some reason known only to themselves, the authorities wished to focus international attention on the new campaign. But the issues were still so carefully disguised that we came away with little impression except that something was afoot. As anyone who has tried it knows, reading a mass of Chinese wall posters while standing in the snow is not an easy business, even if your Chinese is passable, and I wound up with stiff knees and frozen fingers.

It was not until after Chou's death in January, 1976, that the campaign against his protégé became more explicit. In February the posters at Pei-ta denounced Teng by name for the first time. He was linked with Lin Piao and Liu Shao-ch'i, and all were represented as the "horrible three-headed monster". Following pro-Teng riots on T'ien An Men Square in April, the radicals finally prevailed on Mao to dismiss the Deputy Premier, but their victory was to be short-lived. In the wake of Mao's own death five months later, the radicals were swept from power by the army generals and a new campaign began—aimed this time against the so-called "Gang of Four", which was led by Mao's widow, Chiang

A massive mausoleum built to house the embalmed body of Mao Tse-tung rises from a paved concourse in T'ien An Men Square. Completed in July, 1977, ten months after the death of China's venerated leader, the building is a point of pilgrimage for citizens from all over the People's Republic.

Ch'ing, and included Yao Wen-yuan, the country's leading radical propagandist, and two members of the all-important standing committee of the Politburo, Chang Ch'un-ch'iao and Wang Hung-wen. In 1977 Teng rejoined the fold as Deputy Premier, Vice-Chairman of the Communist Party and Chief of Staff of the armed forces, and the villains of yesterday's wall posters became the heroes of today's.

Although the students are obviously manipulated in this process, it would be wrong to imagine that they do not altogether enjoy it. It is highly exhilarating to be a standard-bearer in a national power struggle, even if one has only a vague idea of the issues and personalities involved. Those who were Red Guards in the 1960s often look back on the period with the nostalgia of war veterans recalling their active service. It was a time when the adrenalin really raced through the veins. Besides, students like to vent grievances against their elders and superiors, even if it means staying up all night to write wall posters based on the latest political directive. At the same time, Pei-ta students have shown a certain cynicism about the never-ending sloganeering. Some of these campaigns are tediously repetitive and others blatantly contradictory, but all have a disruptive effect on studies, thus threatening the students' career prospects.

Once, strolling through Pei-ta's lovely grounds with some English friends who had been permitted to study at the university, I experienced one of the more remarkable consequences of "putting politics in command". Passing the picturesque lake, fringed with man-made mounds of stark, bare earth dotted with trees, we approached the traditionally styled Chinese pavilion that housed the university computer. Suddenly, we heard a strange, reedy whine. The computer had been programmed to play an aria from one of the revolutionary Chinese operas that were in vogue at the time. We were more flabbergasted than amused that valuable computer time and a computer research programme should be squandered on the humming of tunes, revolutionary or otherwise.

The life of students at Pei-ta is a regimented pattern of physical exercise, study, political meetings, recreation, food and sleep. An alarm bell rings at 6 a.m., when everyone is supposed to leap out of bed for an early morning run. This is not too difficult to avoid and some students sleep on until breakfast time. Breakfast lasts from 6.40 until 7.30 and is normally followed by four lecture periods of 50 minutes each. The schedule may vary, however, according to the demands of the current political campaign; in recent years, even the regular curriculum has been based on group political discussions rather than formal instruction.

Lunch, which consists usually of steamed bread, rice and vegetables, is served at 11.30 and, after taking a short nap, students start work again at 2 p.m. The afternoon is divided into two lecture periods, but again political meetings may interfere. One afternoon a week is also devoted to physical training. Indeed, the authorities are so concerned with fitness that physically disabled youngsters are not even allowed to attend a university.

The late afternoon is generally free for sport, washing clothes, taking a shower, or writing letters. Dinner is at 6 p.m. and, provided there are no more political meetings, students can spend the rest of the evening reading, chatting, or watching the single-channel television programmes presented by the Peking Broadcasting System. Programmes are devoted mainly to popular science, sports, opera, theatre and children's entertainment, and transmissions rarely last beyond 10.30 p.m.

Students are meant to be in bed by 10 p.m., but many stay up for another two or three hours, studying or just gossiping. Few are prepared to go beyond this in defying the regulations. Pei-ta students are very conscious of their special status and are careful to do nothing that could jeopardize it. Like all young people in China, they must pay particular attention to the taboo against extra-marital sex. Illicit love-making is one of the few crimes the Party does not regard as redeemable; and any couple found in compromising circumstances are liable to be expelled.

Boys and girls still fall in love, however—even at Pei-ta—and where there is love there usually is passion. If the couple restrain themselves and conduct their relationship in a "comradely" manner—studying their homework together, or whispering under a willow tree by the lake—the worst they are likely to suffer is the teasing of their friends. But if they lose control, and the authorities find out, there can be dreadful consequences. One girl jumped to her death from a third-storey window just after attending a meeting called to criticize her conduct, and her "accomplice" was either imprisoned or sent off to a labour camp. Few of their fellow students showed much pity. Although the same stern code officially applies to everyone at Pei-ta, sex is tolerated between members of the university's 300-strong contingent of foreign students, provided couples are discreet. Over past years, however, foreign students have faced a series of political restrictions—presumably because they were not entirely trusted. They were not allowed to read the campus journal, and they could not join the students' union or take part in departmental meetings.

Although a native student can give his foreign room-mate unique insights into Chinese ideas and attitudes, there is no question of a free-and-easy, discuss-all relationship. Even the boldest Chinese are unlikely to be drawn into a critical discussion of their own political system, preferring instead to concentrate on the supposed defects of life in the West. The contempt they express for Western morals and materialism is tinged with envy, however, and envy can easily grow into discontent. Mao hoped to inoculate the younger generation of Chinese against "bourgeois and revisionist" aspirations with massive doses of revolutionary fervour—if necessary "for the next thousand or even ten thousand years". But Mao's successors have abandoned this doctrine as being too disruptive; and if the expectations of young people can no longer be sublimated or diverted, they may have to be fulfilled.

The new leadership has loosened the ideological straitjacket and Peking is becoming a more open place. After Mao's death, the authorities started encouraging foreign tourists to visit the city and took a new interest in restoring old monuments to attract them. But this is certain to be a limited effort. Perhaps alone among the great cities of the world, Peking seems intent on discarding all but a tiny fraction of its past. Whether the future can provide an entirely adequate substitute remains to be seen.

Spectacles of Solidarity

Pupils stand crisply to attention during a Sports Day ceremony at a Peking school. The students dressed in red will carry flags in the opening procession.

One of Peking's hallmarks is a predilection for parades, rallies and other group demonstrations, ranging from modest neighbourhood events to the grandiose spectacles that are held to celebrate major state occasions. In spite of official claims that many of the gatherings are spontaneous exhibitions of popular feeling, they are almost always carefully stage-managed: universities and workplaces may be required to send a quota of "volunteers"; chalk marks on the street are used to position different units; and leaders carry scripts to orchestrate the chanting of slogans. Yet these events are genuinely enjoyed by the city's inhabitants, some of whom form groups to practise marching in their leisure hours. Their enthusiasm is reflected in a precision of execution that turns planned exercises in fraternity into awesome pageants of mass-discipline.

After Mao's death in September, 1976, army units are marshalled on Ch'ang An avenue before joining thousands of civilian workers in T'ien An Men Square.

Soldiers squat behind flags at a rally held in T'ien An Men Square to celebrate the appointment of Mao's successor, Hua Kuo-feng, as Communist Party Chairman.

Women carrying simulated artillery shells march past a mural created by 8,800 flashcard-wielding spectators at the opening ceremony of the National Games.

Bibliography

Adams, Ruth (ed.), *Contemporary China.* Peter Owen, London, 1969.

Ando, Hikotaro, *Peking.* Kondansha International Ltd., Tokyo, 1972.

Arlington, I. C. and Lewisohn, William, *In Search of Old Peking.* Paragon Book Reprint Corporation, New York, 1967.

Bredon, Juliet, *Peking.* Kelly & Walsh, Limited, Shanghai, 1920.

Burchett, Wilfred, with Alley, Rewi, *China: The Quality of Life.* Penguin Books, Harmondsworth, 1976.

Cameron, Nigel, *Barbarians and Mandarins.* Weatherhill, New York, 1970.

Cameron, Nigel, and Brake, Brian, *Peking, a Tale of Three Cities.* Harper & Row, New York, 1965.

Collier, John and Elsie, *China's Socialist Revolution.* Stage 1, London, 1973.

Colombo, Furio, *The Chinese.* Grossman Publishers, New York, 1972.

Dawson, Raymond, *Imperial China.* Hutchinson, London, 1972.

Dunne, George H., *Generation of Giants.* Oates, London, 1962.

Fairbank, John K., Reischauer, Edwin O. and Craig, Albert M., *East Asia, the Modern Transformation.* Allen & Unwin, London, 1967.

Fodor, (ed.), *Peking.* Hodder and Stoughton, 1972.

Fitzgerald, C. P., *China: A Short Cultural History.* Cresset Press, London, 1961.

Hammond, Jonathan, *China, the Land and its People.* Macdonald, London, 1974.

Hinton, William, *Hundred Day War.* Monthly Review Press, London, 1972.

Hsu-Balzer, Eileen, Balzer, Richard J., and Hsu, Francis L. K., *China Day by Day.* Yale University Press, London, 1974.

Kesser, William (ed.), *Childhood in China.* Yale University Press, London, 1975.

Macciochi, Maria Antonietta, *Daily Life in Revolutionary China.* Monthly Review Press, London, 1972.

MacFarquhar, Roderick, *The Forbidden City.* Newsweek, New York, 1972.

Moule, A. C., and Pelliot, Paul, *Marco Polo —The Description of the World.* Routledge, London, 1938.

Orleans, Leo A., *Every Fifth Child: The Population of China.* Eyre Methuen, London, 1972.

Pearl, Cyril, *Morrison of Peking.* Penguin Books, Harmondsworth, 1970.

Polo, Marco, *The Travels.* Penguin Books, Harmondsworth, 1976.

Reischauer, Edwin O. and Fairbank, John K., *East Asia, the Great Tradition.* Allen & Unwin, London, 1958.

Riboud, Marc, *The Three Banners of China.* Collier-Macmillan, London, 1966.

Robinson, Joan, *The Cultural Revolution in China.* Penguin Books, Harmondsworth, 1969.

Robinson, Thomas W. (ed.), *The Cultural Revolution in China.* University of California Press, Berkeley, 1971.

Salisbury, Harrison E., *To Peking—And Beyond.* Arrow Books, London, 1973.

Schram, Stuart, (ed.), *Mao Tse-tung Unrehearsed, Talks and Letters: 1956-71.* Penguin Books, Harmondsworth, 1975.

Schram, Stuart R., *The Political Thought of Mao Tse-tung.* Penguin Books, Harmondsworth, 1969.

Scott, A. C., *Mei Lan-fang.* Hongkong University Press, Hong Kong, 1959.

Shabad, Theodore, *China's Changing Map.* Methuen, London, 1972.

Sirén, Osvald, *The Walls and Gates of Peking.* John Lane, London, 1924.

Sitwell, Osbert, *Escape with Me! An Oriental Sketchbook.* Macmillan & Co. Ltd., London, 1939.

Solomon, Richard H., *Mao's Revolution and the Chinese Political Culture.* University of California Press, London, 1972.

Snow, Edgar, *Red China Today.* Penguin Books, Harmondsworth, 1976.

Snow, Edgar, *The Slow Revolution.* Vintage Books, New York, 1973.

Suyin, Han, *China in the Year 2001.* C. A. Watts & Co. Ltd., London, 1967.

Suyin, Han, *The Morning Deluge, Mao Tsetung and the Chinese Revolution 1893-1953.* Jonathan Cape, London, 1972.

The Times (compiled by), *China's Three Thousand Years.* Times Newspapers Limited, London, 1973.

Thompson, John, *Illustrations of China and its People (4 vols.).* Sampson Low, Marston, Low, and Searle, London, 1873-4.

Thompson, John, *Through China with a Camera.* Harper and Brothers, London, 1899.

Topping, Seymour, *Journey Between Two Chinas.* Harper Colophon Books, London, 1972.

Warner, Marina, *The Dragon Empress.* Cardinal, London, 1974.

Whitaker, Donald P., and Shinn, Rinn-Sup, *Area Handbook for the People's Republic of China.* The American University, Washington D.C., 1972.

Witke, Roxane, *Comrade Chiang Ch'ing.* Weidenfeld & Nicolson, London, 1977.

World Development, *China's Road to Development, Vol. 3, Numbers 7 & 8.* Pergamon Press Ltd., Oxford, 1975.

Worsley, Peter, *Inside China.* Allen Lane, London, 1974.

Yutang, Lin, *Imperial Peking.* Elek Books Limited, London, 1961.

Yutang, Lin, *My Country and My People.* Heinemann, London, 1962.

Acknowledgements and Picture Credits

The author and editors wish to thank the following for their valuable assistance:

Dr. William Atwell, London; Norman Bancroft-Hunt, Caterham on the Hill, Surrey; C. F. Barnes, London; Charles Dettmer, Thames Ditton, Surrey; Dr. John Gardner, Manchester; Susan Goldblatt, London; Liz Goodman, London; Reg Hunt, Oxford; The Royal Geographical Society, London; Society for Anglo-Chinese Understanding, London; Frances Wood, London; Michael Yahuda, London.

Sources for pictures in this book are shown below. Credits for the pictures from left to right are separated by commas; from top to bottom they are separated by dashes.

All photographs are by Peter John Griffiths except: Cover—René Burri from Magnum Photos. Front end paper—Robert McKinley. Page 10, 11—Map by Hunting Surveys Ltd., London. Silhouettes by Norman Bancroft-Hunt. 13—Reg Hunt. 15—Georg Gerster from John Hillelson Agency. 17—Robert McKinley. 18, 19—Reg Hunt. 20—Robert McKinley. 34—(top right) Robert McKinley. 42—Robert McKinley. 45—Richard and Sally Greenhill. 52—Robert McKinley. 58 to 61—Royal Geographical Society, London. 62, 63—School of Oriental and African Studies, London. 64—Royal Geographical Society, London. 65—School of Oriental and African Studies, London. 66—Gunn Brinson. 69—British Museum, London. 71—Christina Gascoigne from Robert Harding Associates, London. 74—Gunn Brinson. 75—Harrison Forman. 79—(inset) Bibliothèque Nationale, Paris. 81—Courtesy of the Smithsonian Institution, Freer Gallery of Art, Washington, D.C. 83—Dr. Jacqueline Ashby. 86, 87—René Burri from Magnum Photos. 91—Bildarchiv Preussischer Kulturbesitz, Kunstbibliothek der Staatlichen Museen Preussischer Kulturbesitz, Bildarchiv, Berlin. 94, 95—Georg Gerster from John Hillelson Agency. 97—P. B. Whitehouse. 101—Reg Hunt. 102, 103—Reg Hunt. 104—(top) Robert McKinley. 106, 107—Marc Riboud from Magnum Photos. 111—Reg Hunt. 112, 113—Reg Hunt. 120—Vittoriano Rastelli. 123—(bottom) Marc Riboud from Magnum Photos. 126—Gunn Brinson. 130-31—Vittoriano Rastelli. 132, 133—Robert McKinley. 135—Robert McKinley. 138—Georg Gerster from John Hillelson Agency. 149—Vittoriano Rastelli. 154—Robert McKinley. 155—Isabel Hilton from John Hillelson Agency—Georg Gerster from John Hillelson Agency. 156—Robert McKinley. 168—Reg Hunt. 170—Alberto Incrocci. 190, 191—Reg Hunt. 196, 197—Stefan from Transworld Feature Syndicate.

Index

Colour reproduction by Irwin Photography Ltd., at their Leeds PDI Scanner Studio.
Filmsetting by C. E. Dawkins (Typesetters) Ltd., London, SE1 1UN.
Printed and bound in Italy by Arnoldo Mondadori, Verona.